DAVID G. ROBB

OGDEN AREA CLIMBING GUIDE
FROM BRIGHAM CITY TO ECHO CANYON

Sharp End Publishing
Authentic Guides From Core Climbers

Ogden Area Climbing Guide: From Brigham City to Echo Canyon
by David G. Robb

Published and distributed by:
Sharp End Publishing, LLC
PO Box 1613
Boulder, CO 80306
t. 303.444.2698
www.sharpendbooks.com

ISBN: 1-892540-38-X converted number is 978-1-892540-38-6

Cover Photos
Top Photo: Brady Anderson projecting on the SR-71 Wall . Photo by David G. Robb
Bottom Photo: Greg Batt on the Lower Roof on the Macabre Wall. Photo by Gary Davis

Book layout by Heidi Knapp and Tara Brouwer.
Cover design by Tara Brouwer, www.TaraBrouwer.com and Heidi Knapp

READ THIS BEFORE USING THIS BOOK
WARNING:

Climbing is a very dangerous activity. Take all precautions and evalu-
ate your ability carefully. Use judgment rather than the opinions
represented in this book. The publisher and author assume no responsibility for injury or death resulting from the use of this book.
This book is based on opinions. Do not rely on information, descriptions, or difficulty ratings as these are entirely subjective. If you are
unwilling to assume complete responsibility for your safety, do not
use this guidebook.

THE AUTHOR AND PUBLISHER EXPRESSLY DISCLAIM ALL REPRESENTATIONS AND
WARRANTIES REGARDING THIS GUIDE, THE ACCURACY OF THE INFORMATION HEREIN,
AND THE RESULTS OF YOUR USE HEREOF, INCLUDING WITHOUT LIMITATION, IMPLIED
WARRANTIES OF MERCHANTABILITY AND FITNESS FOR A PARTICULAR PURPOSE.
THE USER ASSUMES ALL RISK ASSOCIATED WITH THE USE OF THIS GUIDE.

It is your responsibility to take care of yourself while climbing. Seek
a professional instructor or guide if you are unsure of your ability to
handle any circumstances that may arise. This guide is not intended as
an instructional manual.

Dedication

For Ruth, Caleb, and Ethan.

Acknowledgments

When I decided to write a guidebook for this area I had no idea what I was getting myself into. What I thought would be a good excuse to do a lot of climbing, quickly turned into a monstrous project that required more time in front of a computer than outdoors. Well over two years past my original deadline and after countless setbacks. It's hard to believe this book is finally a reality. I could never have done it alone. This book never would have existed if it were not for the tremendous efforts of many people.

Two former guidebooks for the Ogden area provided the foundation for this book. I never would have been able to gather all the information in this book without the previous efforts of Dave Black and Brain Mecham. The St. Joe's Boulderfield guide was selflessly contributed by the indefatigable Brent Hadley who I must also thank for much advice and information.

Countless others provided encouragement, friendship, and valuable information. I would like to thank the following people (in no particular order): Gary Davis who practically co-authored this book and was kind enough to contribute the Geology section, Maury Grimm at Junction Magazine who provided technical know-how and other much needed support, Greg Batt, Brett Fuller, Kelly Oldroyd who patiently endured hours of my ranting, the super-motivated Mike Anderson, the legendary Ken Gygi, Mike Pleinis, Kevin Fosburg who is the only person bold enough to make a habit of climbing in Echo Canyon, Tom Burton, Anthony Chertudi, Paul Booth, Kent Ripplinger who is the only guy I know that stops in the middle of a pitch to jot down a thought in his journal before continuing the climb, Aaron Lyells, Sky Beck, Wayne April, Bruce Roghaar, John Card, Clint Roskelly, and all the guys at Canyon Sports whose incessant pestering kept me motivated, Chris Grijalza, Rob Shaw, Mikel Vause, Bob Ellis, Greg Lowe, Jeff Lowe, the entire Campbell family for hours of babysitting and enthusiastic support, and many others.

More than any one else, I could never have finished this book without help from my family. My brother, Ken, bought an advance copy more than two years before the book was finished and has stood behind me all the way. The encouragement and enthusiasm of my sister, Karen, and my father, Don, has helped to keep me going when I felt like throwing in the towel. My mother, Mary, has helped in every way possible from baby sitting to supplying me with a computer (she is the only person who actually worried more about this book than me). And most of all, my sexy wife, Ruth, with her unending love, patience, and support, is who really made this book happen. Thank you all!

TABLE OF CONTENTS

Introduction

Ogden offers unique experiences and possibilities for climbers. There are several types of rock and routes to choose from, mainly quartzite, limestone, gneiss, and the disconcerting sandstone/conglomerate rock of Echo Canyon. There are alpine style rock climbs in the Willard Spires, easy-access sport routes at 9th Street, hard limestone test pieces at Causey Reservoir, long traditional routes on the Macabre Wall, superb bouldering in St. Joe's boulderfield, and the alluring combination of sport and trad routes overlooking the city on the Schoolroom Wall. There really is something here for everyone.

In addition to the routes you'll find described in this guide book, the mountains around Ogden are filled with lesser known untapped areas that are both mysterious and rugged. These are protected by long steep approaches. Many are hidden in seldom traveled canyons and thick pine forests. They will probably never be listed in any guidebook. These areas offer Ogden climbers something that is swiftly becoming hard to find along the Wasatch: solitude and adventure.

There are, of course, the roadside crags where you'll find grid-bolted rock, and a less committing atmosphere, but I would argue that the best way to experience Ogden climbing is with a desire for exploration. The nature of the rock itself, the geology of the area, and the lack of trails to the crags seems to insist on this kind of approach. With this desire, climbing in Ogden can be incredibly rewarding, without it, the climbing can be limiting and even frustrating.

Ethics

One of the biggest attractions to climbing is that it is a self-governed sport. There are no rules, regulations or referees. There is just yourself, your partner, and a hunk of rock you'd like to get to summit. With this independence comes freedom and responsibility to yourself, other climbers, the community, and the environment. As climbers, we must shoulder these responsibilities and be mindful of the impact of our actions or our sport will not stay self-governed for long.

Above all other aspects of the sport, I value the independence and freedom I find in climbing. The one thing I can't stand is when someone comes along and tries to impose their beliefs about climbing. Thus, I don'tt want to preach about ethics. I do not want to try and tell anyone how I think they should behave. Instead, I will just note a few of climbing's traditional ethics and ask that climbers observe some basic considerations.

There are a few practices that have long been considered unethical by climbers for obvious reasons. Bolts are probably the biggest ethical problem currently facing the Ogden area. Climbers have traditionally limited their placements in two ways:by never place a bolt where natural protection is available, and by never placing a bolt on or within reach of an already existing route. This sounds easy enough, but there is much debate as to what is too close to an existing route and just what can be protected naturally. Probably the best policy is to consider bolts a last resort.

Though not a widespread problem in Ogden, chipping and gluing are major ethical concerns. As with bolt placements, it is considered highly unethical to chip or glue an already existing route. Most climbers agree that you should never chip or glue period. This is definitely the prevailing belief in the Ogden area and the climbing community at large. To those few who see things otherwise, I ask that you please try to detach yourself from the whatever route you are considering chipping and view the situation objectively. Why bring the route down to your level rather than rise to the occasion? Why not see that blank section of rock as a challenge to inspire you to become a stronger and better climber? If you believe the route to be impossible as it is, remember that former generations believed much of what we climb today to be impossible. Why not have the self control to save the rock, unaltered, for future generations? So what if the rock never gets climbed? Why *murder the impossible* as Reinhold Messner put it? If it's glory or recognition you want, remember that nearly all climbers despise chipping and gluing, so you will not become famous, only infamous.

Even if you don't agree with the traditional ideas of ethics, it is important to remember that everybody has a different and very personal vision of climbing. Out of respect for the first ascensionist's vision of his or her route, we should climb it as it is or simply leave it alone. Climbers put a lot of hard work into their routes, and thus can be very protective of them. If you start spraying bolts everywhere and altering existing routes, you certainly won't be very popular and you might get run right out of town.

The last thing I want to mention here is that we need to be protective of the environment. The sport of climbing is growing rapidly and the more climbers there are, the more impact we have on the environment. By doing a few simple things like picking up trash, staying on trails, and cleaning off chalk, we can ensure that we don't ruin the climbing experience for ourselves and others. There are also several Native American pictographs on some of boulders in the Ogden area. Special care needs to be taken not to damage them.

Geology of Ogden's Climbing Areas

By Gary Davis

Ogden is a great area to study various earth science disciplines such as sedimentology, stratigraphy, geomorphology, seismology, petrology, etc. The Geo-Science Department at Weber State University offers classes that teach about these topics. The professors there have ample expertise and interest in the geology of the Ogden area.

The climbing areas of Ogden are part of the Middle Rocky Mountain Physiographic Province which encompasses the mountains in northeastern Utah and parts of Wyoming, including the Tetons. This Province has seen complex uplifting, tilting, folding, and faulting. The rocks in Ogden are quite old. The Farmington Canyon Complex is a crystalline metamorphic rock normally given the name gneiss (pronounced "nice"). The Complex is Precambrian in age, about 1.4 billion years old, and is the only local rock not sedimentary in origin. This rock, in certain places, has many dikes crossing through it often making these areas fun to find minerals. The 9th Street Crag and the lower part of Ogden Canyon are examples of this complex.

The most distinctive formation in Ogden is the Tintic Quartzite. The Tintic spans from north of Brigham City, dominant through Ogden, appears as far south as Provo, and potentially could be spread much further. The Tintic is relatively thick (about 500+ feet locally) and is considered to be a shallow marine deposit of very clean quartz sand. The quartzite is well-cemented, making it quite hard. In many places there are layers with conglomerates up to three to four inches in diameter. This may indicate the Tintic was deposited in an area where extremely strong currents, likely created by a storm, were at work at the time of deposition. Examples of this rock are Schoolroom, 5.8 Wall to Hole in the Rock in Ogden Canyon, Macabre, Nature Center Wall, and The Willard Spires.

Just above the Tintic is the Ophir Shale. Due to its weak nature, there are no climbs in this formation. Shale is generally made up of very small pieces of quartz and micas that have been transported relatively far from their source rock. The bonds between the thin layers of shale are very weak allowing water to enter in between and, therefore, easily weather the rock.

Above the shale is the Maxfield Limestone (technically Dolostone) as seen on Indian Trail, The Blob, The Killer Crag, The Cave, and The Grey Cliffs above the Alaskan Inn in Ogden Canyon. Limestone implies that this deposit was created in the deeper ocean where the only sedimentation is from dying animals and elements/compounds in solution solidifying. By definition, limestone must be 50% calcium carbonate. Calcium carbonate is most often produced by marine animals that secrete this compound to make shells for their protection.

This layering sequence of limestone on top of shale on top of sand (quartzite) represents a large relative rise in sea level in this area at the times of their respective deposition. The division between the Tintic and the Farmington Canyon Complex is an unconformity — a plane where either there was no sediment deposition or there was deposition of sediment but it was eroded away. In both of these cases the result is the same, in that there is a period of time that sediments were not preserved.

photo by Gary Davis

CAMPING:

There is excellent pay camping at Pine View Reservoir at the top of Ogden Canyon, about 15-20 minutes from Ogden City. Most of the sites have nice sandy beaches. To get there take 12th Street east until it takes you into Ogden Canyon. You can't miss the reservoir at the top.

FOOD:

The Oaks located in the middle of Ogden Canyon has decent food and excellent outdoor seating overlooking the river (their breakfast is the best).

If your camping at Pine View or climbing in Causey or Ogden Canyon, you may want to try *Chris's* (7345 E. 900 S. Huntsville on the south side of the reservoir) for burgers or a few drinks.

There are several good restaurants and bars on historic 25th Street. *Roosters* and *The Athenian* are excellent.

COFFEE:

Grounds for Coffee (3005 S Harrison Blvd.), on the east side of Ogden, has excellent coffee and is and is very close to the boulderfield and most of the climbing.

Starbucks (1140 W. Riverdale Rd.) is located close to the freeway and only a few blocks from two of the climbing shops (Canyon Sports and Skimania) and The Wall climbing gym.

EQUIPMENT, GUIDES, & GYMS:

Equipment
Canyon Sports
705 W Riverdale Rd
Riverdale UT 84405
801-621-4662

Ski Mania
4029 Riverdale Rd
Riverdale UT 84405
801-621-7669

Smith and Edwards
3936 N Hwy 126
Farr West UT 84404
801-731-1120

Guides
Exum Utah Mountain Adventures
Black Diamond Center
2092 E 3900 S
Salt Lake City UT 84124

Gyms
Ben Lomond Climbing Center
2370 N Hwy 89
Pleasant View UT 84404
801-737-7274

The Wall
697 W Riverdale Rd
Riverdale UT 84405
801-393-4126

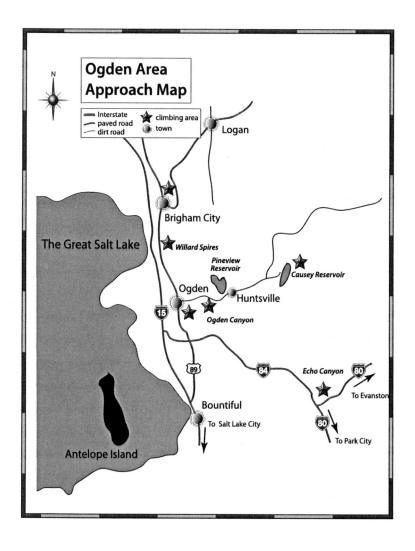

HOW TO USE THIS BOOK

Icons

Approach Information and Time

Easy   Moderate   Difficult   4th Class

Direction Cliff Faces

Sun Exposre

All day sun   All day shade   PM sun   AM sun

Climbing Style

Trad   Sport   Mixed

Bouldering Icons

Bad Landing   Sit Down Start   Highball

Rock Steepness

Slab   Vertical   Steep   Roof

Nature of the Climbng

Crimpy   Powerful   Pumpy   Technical

Star rating System

No Stars = Below average climbing/rock quality
★   Worth the effort
★★   Good route for the crag or area
★★★   Best the crag or area has to offer

BRIGHAM CITY

There are a few areas in and around Brigham City that deserve mention. Much like Ogden, the routes are located on the quartzite cliffbands high on the east bench. All the climbing requires clean gear unless the area can be toproped. Besides the established routes, there are many possibilities for the adventurous trad climber to explore. It should also be mentioned here that there is an extensive amount of untouched limestone in the Honeyville area.

Approach: Take the first Brigham City exit off I-15 to Main Street. Turn right on Main and then left on 700 N. Follow it to where it makes a T with Highland. At this T there is a dirt road that climbs straight up the mountainside to the trailhead. Follow the trail along the stream past the waterfall up to a dirt road that traverses the mountainside. At this point, angle south up the hillside to reach Pyramid Rocks or continue along the stream to reach Karen's Nipple.

___A. Karen's Nipple
This area is located within Brigham City limits just above a cascading little waterfall. This is the most accessible climbing in the area. The climbing here is on a clean quartzite face and ranges from easy to moderate. Leads on the face are bold and sometimes runout. However, the face can be easily toproped by hiking around the right side. Although there are some old fixed pins on top, natural gear will be needed for anchors.

___B. Pyramid Rocks
Hang out with the marmots and enjoy the view. This is a good area for the trad climber who likes the adventure of having no topos or route descriptions, but not too much commitment. The climbs are mostly easy and one or two pitches long.

CHIMNEY ROCK AREA

Chimney Rock is an isolated spire-like boulder standing in the middle of the barren hillside north of Brigham City. The rock quality is excellent and the single route it hosts is the best in the Brigham City area. *One-Legged Loraine* is located on the large cliffband behind (east of) Chimney Rock. There are up to ten other unrecorded routes along this large cliffband. This is another good place for adventurous trad climbers who don't like topos.

Approach: Take I-15 to the north end of Brigham City and take exit #368. Follow 900 N. East and then turn left on Highway 38 heading for Deweyville. Chimney Rock will appear on the right at approximately 2350 North. Park in a small pullout on the right side of the road directly west of the rock. Cross the fence and hike up to the climbs. Access is on privately owned land so be quiet and courteous.

___A. One-Legged Loraine 5.8

This route is seldom climbed and all information on it should be considered as a rough guide only. Look for a detached tower flake in the large alcove directly behind Chimney Rock. Climb third class up to the base of the flake. Climb directly up the face of the flake (5.8) or climb the crack on its left side (5.6). From the top of the tower flake, climb fourth class up to a smooth face with a large diagonal crack. Ascend the crack and pull over the lip up to a large belay cave. Continue up the ridge or descend gullies about 200 feet to the south. Do NOT descend down the large, deep gully to the north.

___B. Chimney Rock 5.10 ★★

The line begins on the west face and then moves onto the south face at a large ledge. It is also possible to start by traversing in from the right on this same ledge and bypass the entire bottom half of the route. Climb the runout but easy (5.8) south face up to a fixed pin. Then jam and lieback your way over the roof to a jug at the rim. The route can be toproped, but the anchor must be built. Take a selection of cams. Walk off.

A. One-Legged Loraine   B. Chimney Rock

B. Chimney Rock

15

HAVE A TOUGH DAY.

Build strength. Improve flexibility, coordination, balance, climbing skill and self-esteem. Each approach to the wall is an opportunity to overcome challenge, to grow and to re-create. It's a good way to focus and toughen up (it's also a blast).

The Ben Lomond Climbing Center offers safe, indoor climbing challenges for both the novice and the extremist: cracks, friction, roofs, under-clings, steep caves, easy faces, over 4,000 square feet of climbing surface and 18 top ropes. It's all here.

BEN LOMOND CLIMBING CENTER

NOTHING'S HOLDING YOU DOWN

(801) 737 7274

Brigham City

2700 North

Exit 352
Plain City
No. Ogden

U.S. 89

0.5 mi.

BLCC
2370 N., HWY 89

2.5 mi.

Larsen Ln.

I-15

N

Wall Ave.

Wash. Blvd.
Ogden

WILLARD SPIRES

The Willard Spires are the rugged and awe-inspiring peaks which overlook Willard Bay north of Ogden. The spires provide alpine style rock climbing, adventure, solitude, and beautiful views — all within a 20 minute drive from Ogden. Be aware that the climbing here is committing and often runout with loose rock and difficult route finding. Approach and descent times vary from two to three hours, so plan on a full day. The approach descriptions found below start from the base of the mountains in or around the city of Willard. However, an alternative for some of the routes is to take a four-wheel drive road up to the back side of the spires from the city of Mantua. It is then possible to descend to the base of the routes and summit near your car. This road is over an hour long and requires a high clearance vehicle. Please note: Although there have been many other routes done in this area, information on most of them was never recorded. Many of the routes listed have unconfirmed ratings, descriptions, and approaches. You must use your best judgement and have a good sense of adventure. Don't go near this place without a helmet. The routes listed are either the best quality or most popular.

Birdie's Wall   London Spire   Super Bowl

Birdie's Wall
pg 19

5.0-5.7	5.8	5.9	5.10	5.11	5.12	5.13	5.14
	1						

London Spire
pg 20

5.0-5.7	5.8	5.9	5.10	5.11	5.12	5.13	5.14
4		2					

The Ogre
pg 24

4th Class	5.7	5.9	5.10	5.11	5.12	5.13	5.14
1	1						

The Prow
pg 25

5.0-5.7	5.8	5.9	5.10	5.11	5.12	5.13	5.14
1	1						

Brady Anderson on The Southwest Ridge, Willard Spires 5.7   Photograph by Troy Lincoln

BIRDIE'S WALL

Birdie's Wall is the prominent northernmost spire just south of Willard Canyon. The *West Face* is currently the only known route on the spire. The approach is up Cook Canyon. To reach it, take Hwy. 89 north to Willard Canyon Road. This road is unmarked, but it is located between an old rock spillway and the Historic Willard Cemetery at approximately 300 North. Follow Willard Canyon Road east until it splits and take the right fork beneath a pipeline. Turn right on the last dirt road just before the gate to the gravel pit and then quickly take a left fork up a small incline. You should now have a canal running along the left side of the road. Follow this dirt road past a fence and along the canal until a gate is reached. Park here and be sure not to block the road or the gate. Cook Canyon is visible to the southeast. It is located directly below the north face of London Spire and Birdie's Wall. Hike along the dirt road past an orchard to the canyon. Plan on at least three hours for this long and difficult approach.

___A. West Face III 5.8
Begin the route by climbing fourth class up to a big dihedral in the center of the wall just below the Super Bowl. Climb the face left of the dihedral (5.8). This is the crux pitch and there is reportedly very little pro. From the Super Bowl, move left and then follow a series of south-facing dihedrals to the summit ridge. Eight or nine pitches.

LONDON SPIRE

London Spire is the prominent spire south of Birdie's Wall. It is the tallest, most obvious, and arguably the most beautiful of the spires. All routes on the north and west faces should use the Birdie's Wall approach. The *Southwest Ridge* and *South Face* should be approached by hiking up Holmes Canyon — the narrow canyon angling southward down from the south face of London Spire. To reach it, park on the side of Hwy. 89 at the "Welcome to Willard" sign located at approximately 6950 South. Hike directly east up the hillside to the mouth of the canyon and be careful not to disturb land owners. Wind your way up Holmes Canyon until the dark brown layer of gneiss meets the quartzite of the upper spire. At this poin,t hike up a steep gully to a notch on the north side of the canyon where the *Southwest Ridge* begins or continue up Holmes Canyon for the *South Face*.

Note: About 20 minutes of approach time can be saved by getting permission from local land owners to use dirt roads that will take you nearly to the mouth of Holmes Canyon. High clearance vehicles will be needed.

___**B. Direct North Face III** 5.9

There are two major variations to this route. The right variation is 5.7 and the left is 5.8. Other variations have been known to make the entire route as easy as 5.7. All variations have runout and hard-to-protect sections, loose rock, and difficult route finding. Do not underestimate this route. The first ascent was a 23-hour epic. It climbs the gullies and faces up the left side of the north face. 10 to 12 pitches.

___**C. Original North Face IV** 5.9

(See Birdie's Wall for photo)

This route also has two major variations. The right variation (5.9) is the original Greg Lowe and Scott Etherington route first climbed in January of 1969. It took three days and was ascended as a practice route for the first winter ascent of the North Face of the Grand Teton. They climbed it all free in temperatures estimated to be as low as -30 degrees with wind chill. The left variation is 5.7. The route follows several gullies and faces to the left of the *Northwest Ridge* on the right side of the north face. Near the top it angles left and connects with the *Direct North Face*. 15 to 20 pitches.

Brady Andersen on Southwest Ridge   Photograph by Troy Lincoln

___**D. Northwest Ridge III** 5.7
(See Birdie's Wall for photo)
Plan on some dirty loose climbing.
Ten pitches

___**E. West Face III** 5.7
(Also see Birdie's Wall photo)
The west face is one of the most scenic
routes in the area. Unfortunately, the rock
is often rotten. Ten pitches.

___**F. Southwest Ridge III** 5.7 ★
This is as near as it gets to a Willard Spires
classic. Begin in a saddle at the base of the
ridge where the dark brown layer of gneiss
meets the quartzite of the spire. The route
follows the ridgeline for its entire length.
About two-thirds of the way up the ridge
is a large shelf called the Lunch Ledge. Just
before this ledge is the crux (5.7) pitch.
Most of the route is easy fifth class. Ten
pitches.

___**G. South Face III** 5.7
The route begins in an obvious alcove and
ascends the center of the south face. It
joins the *Southwest Ridge* at Lunch Ledge.
Eight pitches.

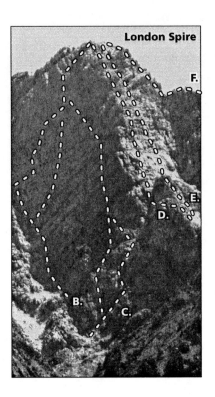

London Spire

London Spire, Southwest Ridge

London Spire, West Face

THE OGRE

The Ogre is the southern most spire. It has the shortest routes, but some of the longest approaches. These approaches vary depending on the route. The extremely long and strenuous approach is up Pearson's Canyon south of the peak. You must get permission from local land owners to gain access to the canyon.

___A. The Great Book II 4th Class

This route is located on the giant, right-angling dihedral on the Ogre's west face. Approach up Pearson's Canyon on the north side of the peak. Once near the base of the Orge, climb up out of canyon to the ridge that divides the north and south sides of the spire. This ridge drops steeply off to the south and you must either rappel or downclimb to the start of the route.

___B. South Face II 5.5

This unconfirmed route climbs for three pitches up the broken, dirty, and vegitation-covered south face of the Ogre. Approach up the unnamed canyon south of the Ogre. It is the next major canyon south of Pearson's. The canyon forks several times but you always take the left fork. Plan on 4th or 5th class climbing on the approach.

THE PROW

The Prow is a smaller buttress in the canyon south of The Ogre. Approach as for the south face of the Orge, but take the righthand fork of the canyon. This is another long and difficult approach with a 50-foot 5.6 pitch after the righthand fork.

___C. Prow Center II 5.8 ★

This unconfirmed routes is said to have some of the best climbing in the Willard Spires. It climbs three to four pitches up the left side of the prow's southwest face. There is no obvious line, so plan on linking discontinuous and horizontal cracks.

___D. Prow Right II 5.7

This route is very similar to *Prow Center*, but it climbs the ritht side of the prow's soutwest face.

Williard Spires in winter

WEBER HIGH BOULDER

The Weber High Boulder is located in an area where a lot of housing development is taking place. It is currently only yards away from the back yard of one of the new houses. When climbing here be sure to be quiet, courteous, and keep a low profile, otherwise the area may be permanently closed. The routes are located on the south side of a giant quartzite boulder. They are easily accessible and can be toproped. Presently there are only two routes, but room for more exists on the impressive west face. Poison ivy is plentiful around the climbs, so be careful.

Approach: From the intersection of 12th Street and Washington Blvd. take Washington Blvd. north. Turn left on Elberta Street (2850 N.) and then right on 500 W. Take 500 W. until you turn right again on 3950 N. Follow this street until it dead ends at a dirt road. The boulder can be seen directly behind the last house on the north side of the road. Park at the dead end and then walk up the dirt road around and behind the house. The routes are on the south face of the boulder. Remember to be quiet and courteous.

___ **A. High Velocity Wrench** 5.11a ★
Pumpy and strenuous climbing up the left arête of the boulder. Start off the boulder to the left or traverse in from *Inverted Insertion*. The first bolt is a little high and it has only one bolt for the anchor. Take long runners for the anchor if you plan to toprope. Three bolts.

___ **B. Inverted Insertion** 5.11b ★
A pumpy line up the center of the face. The first bolt is high and there are sporty gaps between the others. It might be possible to get in some natural pro. The anchor consists of one bolt and two widely spaced pitons. Two bolts.

THE NATURE CENTER WALL

The Nature Center Wall is a large and vastly diverse area comparable to The Schoolroom. The approaches are moderately long and strenuous, but climbers are rewarded with solitude and a beautiful view. This long quartzite cliffband stretches from the Sun Deck all the way to the Macabre Gully. It has been broken into six different areas: The Sun Deck, The Big Deck, the SR-71 Wall, the Couch Surfing Area, the Big Jake Wall, and the Madison Wall. The areas are listed from north to south. There are many excellent routes for both the sport climber and crack climber.

Approach: Besides this general approach description, each area will have an individual description as well. From the intersection of Harrison Blvd. and 12th Street, take Harrison Blvd. for 2.6 miles north to the Mountain Road Nature Center. This is approximately 1200 N. Harrison Blvd. Park in the Nature Center parking lot and take the trail heading east. The trail angles north up the hillside and then forks. Head left for the areas on the north end of the wall. For the southern end, switchback to the right. Refer to the individual area approach descriptions for more information.

NORTH OGDEN OVERVIEW

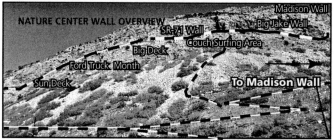

NATURE CENTER WALL OVERVIEW

The Sun Deck pg 28	5.0-5.7	5.8	5.9	5.10	5.11	5.12	5.13	5.14

The Sun Deck: I (5.10), I (5.11)

The Big Deck pg 30	5.0-5.7	5.8	5.9	5.10	5.11	5.12	5.13	5.14

The Big Deck: 2 (5.11), 2 (5.12)

SR-71 Wall pg 32	5.0-5.7	5.8	5.9	5.10	5.11	5.12	5.13	5.14

SR-71 Wall: 4 (5.8), I (5.9)

Couch Surfing Area pg 35	5.0-5.7	5.8	5.9	5.10	5.11	5.12	5.13	5.14

Couch Surfing Area: I (5.8), I (5.9), I (5.11), I (5.12)

Big Jake Wall pg 37	5.0-5.7	5.8	5.9	5.10	5.11	5.12	5.13	5.14

Big Jake Wall: I (5.13)

THE SUN DECK

00:35

The Sun Deck has two high quality sport routes which are well worth a visit. Since you pass this area on the way to the north end of the Nature Center Wall, the routes here serve as great warm-ups for some of the harder routes above. The wall faces west getting morning shade and afternoon sun.

Approach: The Sun Deck is not actually part of the Nature Center Wall. Rather, it is on a small detached cliffband halfway up the hillside to the main wall. To reach it, follow the trail east from the Nature Center parking area. It soon angles north up the hillside and then forks at a switchback. Take the lefthand trail and follow it to the north along the mountainside. As you hike, use the powerline poles highest on the hill for reference. When you are between the second and third powerline poles (including the one at the fork), watch for a cairn built on top of a small boulder. This indicates where to cut up the hillside. There is no real trail to speak of from this point on. Angle continuously up and south following the cairns up the steep, loose slope until the Sun Deck is reached. Approach time is about 35 minutes.

The Sun Deck

___**A. Forearm Foreplay** 5.11a ★

A steep four-bolt route on mostly large holds. Plan on a good pump.

___**B. Featured Fantasy** 5.10c ★

A very similar route to *Forearm Foreplay*, but not quite as relentless. Four bolts.

___**C. Ford Truck Month** (project)

This route is not actually on the Sun Deck. It is located uphill and to the south on a large boulder on the way to the Big Deck. This short boulder problem has yet to be redpointed. It climbs the overhanging west face of the boulder and is estimated to be 5.13c. Three bolts and a single-bolt anchor. Not pictured.

THE BIG DECK

The Big Deck is an excellent sport climbing area located on the north end of the Nature Center Wall. This is a good place to go if you're tired of 9th Street and looking for a new challenge. The approach is long, steep, loose and strenuous. A stick-clip is recommended for most of the routes.

Approach: Follow the approach description for the Sun Deck and then continue hiking up hill and slightly to the south. Aim for the big, west-facing, overhanging boulder where *Ford Truck Month* is located. Traverse beneath the boulder and then begin angling up and south again. This time aim for a tall spire-like boulder located just below the main Nature Center Wall. The Big Deck is directly above the tall boulder. Approach time is approximately 45 minutes.

___**A. Jump Start** 5.11c R
This is the three-bolt route on the far left. Anticipate campus moves on sharp holds until it eases up at the third bolt. There is a missing bolt between the second and third bolts with likely groundfall potential.

___**B. White Trash** 5.12a ★★
Traverse up the ramp on the left to the first bolt and then enjoy the steep, open-handed, and pumpy climbing above. Five bolts.

___C. Porch Mode 5.12b ★★★

Long crimpy moves lead to a sloper crux on this quartzite classic. This is possibly the best route of its grade in all of Ogden. Five bolts.

___D. Grease Monkey 5.11d

Don't bother with this one unless you've already done every other route on the Big Deck. Four bolts.

Tim Nyugen giving the finger crack project a go on the SR-71 Wall   *Photo by David G. Robb*

SR-71 WALL

This area is where most of the traditional climbing on the Nature Center Wall is concentrated. It is an excellent place for intermediate trad climbers to hone their skills at multiple pitch routes that require setting belays. Helmets are recommended.

Approach: Approach as for The Big Deck and then hike a short distance to the south along the cliff base. The area is easily recognized by the prominent arête on which *Aunt Lulu* is located.

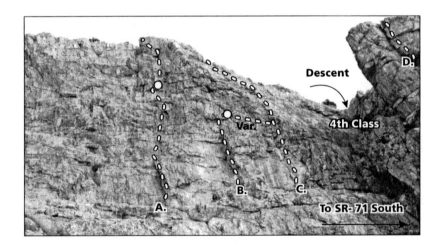

___**A. SR-71** 5.8+ ★

Although this is a worthwhile route, it shares very few of the graceful characteristics usually attributed to the jet for which it is named.

Pitch 1: Climb the obvious dihedral up to a series of ledges. Then pull a short overhanging fist crack to reach the belay.

Pitch 2: This pitch is a little loose and climbs another dihedral above the belay before angling left to the top. The anchor must be built. Take a standard free rack.

Descent: Walk down the obvious gully south of the route. Some fourth class downclimbing will be necessary.

___B. Bumblebee Rumble 5.8 ★★

This is the crack in the back of a small dihedral just right of *SR-71*. It is named for a skirmish that took place between the first ascensionists and a swarm of hornets. The route climbs a very thin finger crack using fun and challenging stemming techniques. Belay on top of the dihedral where there are three fixed pitons. Take a standard free rack with some extra small TCUs. Rappel the route.

___C. Alzheimer's Serpent 5.8 R ★

The crack at the back of a dihedral right of *Bumblebee Rumble*. This 100-foot pitch has a little of everything. Interesting stemming and a hand crack lead up to a loose crux 25 feet up, comprised of steep blocks . The face above has fun 5.7 moves on good edges, but is sparsely protected. Build an anchor on top and descend as for *SR-71*.

___D. Aunt Lulu 5.9 ★★★

Two pitches of quality crack climbing. This is one of the best natural lines on the Nature Center Wall.

Pitch 1: Climb a thin finger crack up to a ledge. From the ledge, climb straight up the short arête or take the easy way out to the right. Belay on The Balcony.

Pitch 2: Climb the beautiful hand crack in the back of the prominent slot. Just before the top, the crack turns into a steep exciting offwidth. Take a standard free rack as well as some extremely small TCUs to protect the start.

Descent: Head down the gully directly behind the route. Some fourth class downclimbing is necessary.

___E. The Thing 5.8 ★★

 The crack system to the right of *Aunt Lulu*. Begin in a pretty fun crack. Jam and face climb up to an unexpected bulge. Pull the bulge and belay on The Balcony. The second pitch climbs the obvious chimney. This V-shaped slot has a nice hand crack in the back for pro and involves fun and creative climbing on jugs.

___F. Project

The overhanging finger crack to the right of *The Thing*.

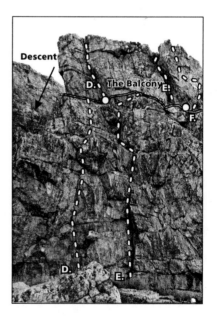

Gary Davis on Long-legged Girls and Fun 5.11b   Photograph by David G. Robb

COUCH SURFING AREA

The Couch Surfing Area, located in the very center of the Nature Center Wall, offers both sport and trad routes. It also hosts some of the only afternoon shade in the area.

Approach: Take the trail east from the Nature Center parking area. It soon angles north up the hillside and then forks at a switchback. Take the right-hand fork and head south. At the second switchback, leave the trail and begin the rigorous hike straight up the scree field. The area is easily recognized by the enormous arête in the center of the cliffband. A longer, yet easier, approach is to follow the approach description for the SR-71 Area and then continue traversing south along the cliff base.

___**A. Closet Cowboy** 5.8
This is the hand crack on the left side. It shares a bolt anchor with *Couch Surfing*. Take a standard free rack.

___**B. Couch Surfing** 5.12a ★★
This route is much steeper than it appears. It's composed of hard, crimpy climbing that continuously angles to the left. Watch out for rope drag if you lower or toprope. Five bolts.

___**C. Black's Crack** 5.9
Righthand crack in the corner. It shares a bolt anchor with *Couch Surfing*. Take a standard free rack.

COUCH SURFING AREA RIGHT

___**D. Fast Cars and Whiskey**
(project)
When eventually redpointed, this
will likely be the hardest route on the
Nature Center Wall. Four bolts. A high
first bolt begs a stick-clip.

___**E. Long-legged Girls and Fun**
5.11b ★★
This distinct route climbs the beauti-
fully exposed arête. Six bolts.

BIG JAKE WALL

The Big Jake Wall supports two sport routes of moderate value. There is potential for more routes of high difficulty near this area.

Approach: Follow the approach description for The Couch Surfing Area, and then traverse south along the cliff base. This is one of the more difficult areas to recognize due to the lack of obvious features, so keep your eyes open or you may walk right on past.

___**A. Puking Pumpkin (project)** ★
This is a quality route that would have received more stars if it were not for a large ledge between the first and second bolts. The crux includes matching on a slippery fin and dynoing right to a jug. The route will probably be 5.12d or 5.13a when it's finally redpointed. Five bolts.

___**B. Big Jake 5.12c** ★
Dynamic climbing along the left-angling corner. It's a little runout to the anchor. Five bolts.

THE MADISON WALL

The Madison Wall is located at the south end of the Nature Center Wall where the cliffband makes a sharp turn straight up the mountainside into the Macabre descent gully. The rock here is south-facing and currently hosts only a handful of routes, although it is likely that more will soon go up.

Approach: Take the trail east from the Nature Center parking area (pg 27). It soon angles north up the hillside and then forks at a switchback. Take the righthand fork and head south. The trail will switchback a few more times and then traverse the hillside to the south. Stay on this trail until directly below the Madison Wall where the trail passes beneath a large pine tree. At this point, cut straight up the talus field to the notch between the brown-colored gneiss on the right and the southern corner of the Nature Center wall on the left.

The Brain
pg 39

5.0-5.7	5.8	5.9	5.10	5.11	5.12	5.13	5.14

Middle Madison Wall
pg 40

5.0-5.7	5.8	5.9	5.10	5.11	5.12	5.13	5.14

Upper Madison Wall
pg 41

5.0-5.7	5.8	5.9	5.10	5.11	5.12	5.13	5.14

To Macabre Descent Gully

Upper Madison Wall

Middle Madison Wall

A.
B.-D.

THE BRAIN

The Brain currently has four sport routes on a unique type of quartzite with more to go in soon. All climbs are located on the west end of the Madison Wall where it forms a corner with the Nature Center Wall.

___**A. Unnamed** 5.10d ★★
Overhanging jug haul. Four bolts.

___**B. Frontal Lobotomy** 5.11d ★
More jugs. Seven bolts.

___**C. Subderal Hematoma**
5.11b ★★★
Still more jugs. Six bolts

___**D. Medulla Oblongata** 5.11a ★
You guessed it, more jugs. Five bolts.

MIDDLE MADISON WALL

There is only one route here, but it's worthwhile if your in the area. To reach The Middle Madison Wall, continue uphill past The Brain. Soon an alcove will appear on the left. *Give Me a Bucket* is the short but nice looking crack at the back of the alcove to the right of a notch.

___**E. Give Me a Bucket** 5.10a ★★
This is an excellent hand crack and would have received a third star if it were a little longer. Start off of the grassy shelf below the route and climb a broken slab up to the beginning of the crack. The anchor on top is a little tricky to build. Take a full selection of cams because there are no adequate nut placements. Scramble off (fourth class) and descend down the chimney to the west. There are other good toprope routes on this same wall.

Descent

UPPER MADISON WALL

For the Upper Madison Wall, continue uphill to where some big overhangs are visible on the left. Just past the overhangs is another alcove. *Search and Rescue* is in the alcove on a dark red, east-facing wall. There is a big notch in the cliffband to the right of the route. It is the only route in this area, but it is well worth the hike.

___**F. Search and Rescue** 5.10 ★★★
The first ascensionist named this route after an adventure he had one night while climbing in the area. Apparently people in the houses below had seen his headlamp and assumed the worst. As it turns out, he soon found himself the object of a rescue he didn't need. It's good to know Weber County Search and Rescue is on the ball.

Begin the route by stemming your way up the nice hand and finger crack in the corner until it ends at a roof and then step out right onto the face. The upper face consists of thin involved moves between one fixed pin and a bolt. The crux finish at the very top makes this an arousing lead. Take a standard free rack.

Descent: Rappel

MACABRE WALL

The Macabre Wall is holy ground for the trad climbers of Ogden. This 500-foot wall is home to the infamous Macabre Roof as well as some of the best multiple pitch climbing around. The dictionary definition for the word "macabre" reads: "Suggesting the horror of death and decay; gruesome; ghastly." There is no doubt, when staring up at the monstrous Macabre Roof looming over you with more than 400 feet of air below your toes, these words describe the feelings you have. On the other hand, while the roof is truly terrifying, it is equally inspiring.

Amazingly, this 40 foot roof was first free climbed by Greg Lowe in 1967 before sticky rubber shoes and camming devices! The roof was originally aided by Greg's brother, Jeff, who bet Greg five dollars he couldn't free it. After which, Greg promptly onsighted the roof with only questionable pitons for pro. Despite many attempts, it took 35 years before the roof was repeated in 2002 by Ken Gygi.

Due to the complexity of the wall, only the original Macabre route with a few of its variations is described. However, there are dozens of routes and every route has dozens of variations, so be adventurous and have fun. All anchors must be built, and good route-finding skills are a must. The routes here are vague at best with long pitches and loose rock. It should be noted that there has actually been one death attributed to the loose rock on this wall. Wear a helmet and be careful.

Approach: The wall is easily visible from the Jump Off Canyon parking lot. Follow the approach description for Jump Off Canyon (pg 46) up to the canal road. Hike north along the road until it dead ends. The trail climbs straight up and slightly north until it disappears into the scree. Follow the scree field up to its apex where most of the routes begin.

Descent: Hike and downclimb the gully to the north. There is some fourth class downclimbing that gets a little scary. Another option is to descend along the north ridge of the gully before eventually downclimbing a fourth class chimney next to *Search and Rescue* (see Madison Wall).

Greg Batt on the Lower Roof of the Macabre Wall   5.6 - 5.12b   Photograph by Gary Davis

___A. Macabre Wall III

5.6-5.12b ★★★

This is The Ogden classic for trad climbing. If you only do one route in Ogden, make it this one. The original Lowe route starts at the very apex of the scree field where a right-facing dihedral forms a roof 50 feet up.

Pitch 1: Climb the face right of the dihedral up to an excellent hand crack which splits the roof. Pull the five-foot roof (5.10) and continue up to a big belay ledge.

Pitch 2: Look for a big, eight-foot overhang with a splitter hand crack about 80 feet above and a little to the right. Climb low-angle faces and cracks (5.6) aiming straight for the roof. Jam your way out the beautiful, yet intimidating, overhang (5.10+) and belay on a ledge just above.

Pitch 3: Angle up and to the right over easy ground (5.6 or less) until the Foops Roof comes into view. Belay on a grassy, relaxing ledge just below the roof.

Pitch 4: The overhangs just keep getting bigger and better. Jam your way over this unrelenting monster and belay below the Macabre Roof (5.11).

Pitch 5: Had enough? If so, bypass the Macabre Roof by traversing right and two more easy pitches will put you on top. If not, climb the crack and flake system on the right side of the roof. Some fixed pins will help guide the way. Located halfway out an overhang is a giant detached flake, that somehow defies gravity. Follow this flake, continu-

ing up the crack out to the right for ten more feet to a belay in a little alcove with some old fixed pins. Cams are all that will go in the roof. Watch out for bad rope drag (5.12b).

Pitch 6: Easy climbing to the top.

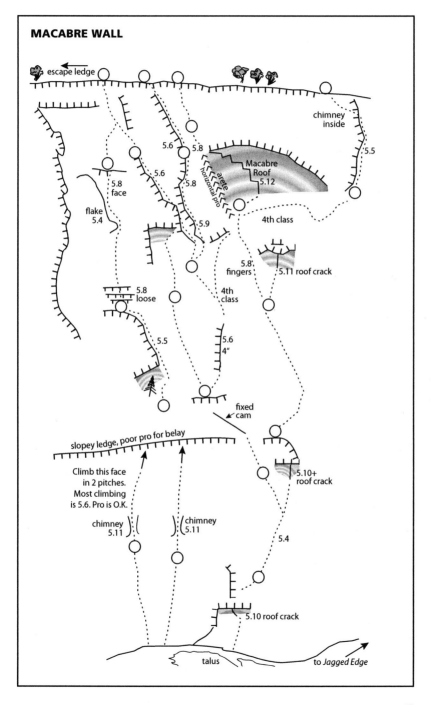

MACABRE WALL

escape ledge

chimney inside

5.5

5.6 5.8

Macabre Roof
5.12

arete
horizontal pro

5.8 face

5.6

5.8

flake 5.4

5.9

4th class

5.8 fingers

5.11 roof crack

5.8 loose

4th class

5.5

5.6
4"

fixed cam

slopey ledge, poor pro for belay

Climb this face in 2 pitches. Most climbing is 5.6. Pro is O.K.

chimney 5.11

chimney 5.11

5.10+ roof crack

5.4

5.10 roof crack

talus

to *Jagged Edge*

JUMP OFF CANYON

The rugged and little-known Jump Off Canyon is located just south of The Macabre Wall. This is a good place to go if you're looking for seclusion or an interesting hike. There are only a handful of established routes in the area, but many possibilities exist for an open-minded and creative climber.

Approach: From the intersection of 12th Street and Harrison, drive north on Harrison to the Jump Off Canyon trailhead located at approximately 495 N. Harrison Blvd. Follow the trail east through a few switchbacks up the hillside to the canal road. Walk north along the canal road until the canal disappears underground. At this point take a trail that cuts up the hillside on the right and into the canyon. See the individual area approach descriptions for more information.

Jagged Edge Area
pg 46

3	2	I					
5.0-5.7	5.8	5.9	5.10	5.11	5.12	5.13	5.14

Jeepers Creepers Area
pg 48

			I				
5.0-5.7	5.8	5.9	5.10	5.11	5.12	5.13	5.14

The Mezzanines
pg 49

3							
5.0-5.7	5.8	5.9	5.10	5.11	5.12	5.13	5.14

JAGGED EDGE AREA

This area is located on the cliffs surrounding the obvious and striking arête on the north side of the mouth of the canyon. There is a wide variety of moderate multi-pitch trad routes. Follow the approach description for the *Unnamed Sport Route A*, then angle up the hillside to the north. Approach time is around 30-35 minutes. All anchors must be built and route-finding skills are a must. Descend via a scary and exposed fifth class downclimb to the east (see photo) or down the Macabre descent to the north (see Macabre Wall, pg 41).

Jagged Edge Area Overview

___A. Unnamed Sport 5.8 (no photo)

This is the only sport route in the canyon. It is located on an obvious brown cliffband rising out of the riverbed. Hike up the main trail along the bottom of the canyon until the crag appears on the left. Approach time is about 10-15 minutes from the car. This lonely sport route isn't too bad, but it's only worth doing if you're on your way to some of the other routes in the area. Four bolts.

___B. Jagged Edge 5.4 ★
This route ascends the main arête. There are a few alternate starts to choose from. Three pitches.

___C. Dirty Dingus McGee 5.9
This route is a more difficult alternate start to *Jagged Edge*. Climb one dirty pitch and then connect with *Jagged Edge*.

___D. Eagle's Roost 5.8 ★
One of the best routes in the area, but you have to get through two pitches of marginal rock to get to the good stuff. Four pitches.

___E. Unnamed 5.6
Four pitches.

___F. Unnamed 5.6
Four pitches.

JEEPERS CREEPERS AREA

Jeepers Creepers is located an additional 30 minutes hike from *Jump Off Sport Route* (see Jump Off Canyon approach, pgs 46,47) at the very back of the canyon where it dead-ends at a small waterfall (usually dry).

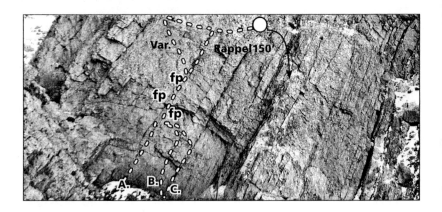

___**A. Jeepers Creepers** 5.10 ★
This route epitomizes the paradox of Ogden trad climbing: a long, strenuous approach to a difficult route of questionable quality, bad and/or tricky gear placements, rattley fixed pins, loose rock, solitude, and a lot of cussing. Yet, for some unexplained reason, when a few days have gone by you think back and say, "Wow, what a great route." Take a standard free rack and some extra runners. The route starts 20 yards right of the dry waterfall. There are three options for the first pitch. All options meet at the same anchor.
Pitch 1:
Option I: Fun, diagonal climbing with intricate foot work.
Option II: Pull the small roof 20 feet up (5.9).
Option III: take the arête to the right of the small roof before angling back left to the anchor (5.7).
Pitch 2: Pull the big roof directly over the belay (5.10). There are some fixed pins, but they are not to be trusted. Although the crux is the roof, don't think it's over after the initial moves. Follow the crack system angling up and right to a grassy ledge. Another unconfirmed variation goes straight up and left shortly after the roof.
Descent: Travese right along the ledge to a big horn and rapel (150 feet).

THE MEZZANINES

The Mezzanines are the huge broken cliffs above the foothills north of Ogden Canyon. This long quartzite cliffband stretches from 350 South to Jump Off Canyon. The Mezzanines have been largely ignored over the years because of their loose and tiered appearance as well as steep approaches. However, good quality trad routes can be found here. There have been dozens of routes done on these cliffs over the years, but none have ever been recorded. The routes listed here are only a small sampling of the possibilities. All the routes require natural pro and all anchors must be built. The route descriptions and ratings are vague to say the least, so go up there with a sense of adventure, a sense of humor, and some good route-finding skills. Helmets are a must.

Approach: Depending on what part of the cliffband you plan to climb, trailheads can be found at the east end of Douglas (350 S.), the corner of Polk (1400 E.) and Cook (150 S.), and the east end of Earl (175 N.). From these trailheads it will be easy to reach the canal road, but from the canal there are no real trails leading up to the base of the cliffs. You simply have to hike straight up (welcome to Ogden).

Descent: Descend down the canyon to the south (above 7th Street) or down the steep gully left of the nose. Both ways will require some third class downclimbing and a rappel or two.

The Mezzanines **pg 50**	3							
	5.0-5.7	5.8	5.9	5.10	5.11	5.12	5.13	5.14

___A. The Nose 5.6

Easy climbing up the obvious prow, with lots of good ledges.

___B. Timex 5.7 ★

This route follows the south face of the prominent buttress centered between *The Nose* and The Amphitheater. Three to four pitches.

___C. Bonington 5.7 ★

This route and *Timex* have the notoriety of first being climbed by Mikel Vause and world renowned mountaineer Chris Bonington. It climbs the south face of the buttress left of The Amphitheater. It is probably the most consistent route on the wall. Three to four pitches.

9TH STREET

Here you have all the elements of modern sport climbing: a short approach, a grid-bolted hunk of steep rock, a broad range of route difficulty, and crowds. The popularity of this place is unrivaled by any other area covered in this book. This popularity is swiftly destroying the mountainside around the crag. On my last visit, there was trash on the ground, severe erosion of trails and the smell of human feces coming from nearby bushes where scraps of toilet paper could be seen. Please help in the upkeep of this area by picking up trash and using the approach mentioned below.

Approach: Park at the east end of 9th Street where it dead-ends at a gate. The crag is visible to the east. Take the gravel road as it angles south up the hill until it connects with the canal road. Turn left on the canal road and then take the first trail angling up the hill on the right. Please avoid the trail that climbs straight up to the crag due to erosion.

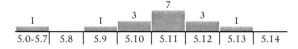

9th Street
pg 53

	I		I	3	7	3	I	
5.0-5.7	5.8	5.9	5.10	5.11	5.12	5.13	5.14

Gibbon Man Cave
pg 56

					I	I project	
5.0-5.7	5.8	5.9	5.10	5.11	5.12	5.13	5.14

Jared on Edge of Madness 5.11c   Photograph by David G. Robb

9TH STREET WEST

___**A. Shino** 5.9 ★
Mostly jugs and positive crimps. If you move to the right around the overhang between the second and third bolts it's 5.8, whereas straight up is 5.9. It's a little sporty from the last bolt to the anchor. Three bolts.

___**B. Cub Scout Corner** 5.6
A good easy toprope for scoutmasters to showoff for the troop.

___**C. Midnight Cowboy** 5.10d ★★
Excellent, uninterrupted climbing up a series of strenuous crimpers. There is an awkward move just before the anchor that has spit off many an exhausted climber after pulling over the crux. The crux is at the third bolt. Three bolts.

___**D. Mr. Interruptus** 5.10c ★★
This is a fun climb with unique moves. Pulling the roof to the anchor is exhilarating. Be sure to take a couple of TCUs to protect the start. It shares an anchor with *Midnight Cowboy*. One piton, one bolt, and natural pro.

___**E. Bolt Sandwich** 5.10c ★
Start as for *Jerusalem* and then move left to the first bolt. The crux is after the first bolt followed by jugs to the top. It shares anchors with *Jerusalem*. Three bolts.

___**F. Jerusalem** 5.11a ★★
Pull the roof using several buckets. Then, ease your way up the corner with tricky, balance-oriented moves. The crux lurks between the second and third bolts. Four bolts.

9TH STREET WEST

___G. Cracked Lip 5.11c ★★★

To make a short wall long — traverse. Very pumpy, sideways climbing on jugs makes this a 9th Street classic. Be aware that this route tends to dominate the wall, and gets in the way of anyone wanting to climb *Jerusalem, Cleft Lip,* or *Vile of Crack.* Be courteous of other climbers. Five bolts.

___H. Cleft Lip 5.11b ★

This route was only recently dubbed *Cleft Lip* since the original name is unknown. Start as for *Cracked Lip* and then climb straight up at the third bolt. The crux is on the upper face where some tenuous and delicate moves must be surpassed to reach the anchor. Five bolts.

___I. Vile of Crack 5.11b/c ★★★

This is one of the best routes 9th Street has to offer. Very steep, strenuous, and pumpy climbing on crimpers and interspersed big holds. One piton and four bolts.

Note: Routes J.-M. all share the final two bolts and the anchor.

___J. Like Pull'n Teeth 5.12.d/13a ★★

This route shares the start of *Vile of Crack* before making a difficult traverse to the right at the second bolt. The crux consists of pulling over the upper bulge on bad crimps and slopers. Very sustained climbing for six bolts and one piton.

9TH STREET EAST

___**K. Project** 5.13d?
Five bolts.

___**L. T.H.C.** 5.12c ★
Three bolts.

___**M. Hankerin'** 5.12b/c
Small crimps on nearly featureless rock.
Four bolts.

___**N. Crank Addiction** 5.11b
This cruxy route has three or four hard
moves that lead to an easy and runout
face above. The crux consists of a hard
throw between the first and second
bolts. This makes it critical to have a
good belayer to keep you out of the
dirt. Three bolts.

___**O. Crank Addiction Direct Finish**
5.11c
This is the direct finish to *Crank Addiction* which branches left at the second
bolt. Five bolts.

___**P. Edge of Madness** 5.11c ★
Analytical climbing on thin edges that
will test your balance and creativity.
Don't get frustrated, the crux is at the
bottom and the route gets easier as it
goes. Four bolts.

GIBBON MAN CAVE

The Gibbon Man Cave is a small overhanging crag a short distance from 9th Street. It is home to one completed route and one project. Unfortunately, the cave is also used by partiers who have left the rock covered in soot and the ground blanketed with broken glass. Please help by packing out any trash you can when in the area.

Approach: Approach as for 9th Street. Upon reaching the canal road, take the second trail angling north up the hillside instead of the first. This trail will pass just beneath 9th Street as it continues north. A short distance later The Gibbon Man Cave will show up on the right.

___**A. Gibbon Man** 5.13? (project)
Although this route has yet to be red-pointed, it is obvious from numerous attempts that the steep thin holds offer decent climbing. From the second bolt it's 5.12b, but the initial moves have never been linked. Six bolts.

___**B. Diagonal Man** 5.12a/b
There are no anchors for this route so the leader must walk off. Four bolts.

Dave G. Robb on Air Time 5.10c   Photograph by Aaron Lyells

OGDEN CANYON

Ogden Canyon is full of great climbing that's only a minute or two from the city. Some of the best climbers in the world have left footprints here. Routes were recorded as early as the 1940s. It offers three types of rock, a huge variety of climbs, and beautiful scenery all within only four miles. The road through the canyon is narrow and winding, so be careful when driving and hiking along it.

All mileage is indicated by each individual area's approach description and starts from the waterfall located on the north side of the mouth of the canyon. Often in late summer, the waterfall is not running so if you are new to the area just start all mileage from the big pullouts just past the suspended pipeline running across the mouth of the canyon.

The maps of the canyon are not to scale, so careful attention to the mileage is highly recommended. Much of the climbing is concentrated in a small and confusing network of steep side gullies within the first mile of the canyon. Many of the areas require that you note the crag as you drive by, park up canyon, and then walk back down. If you have never climbed in this area before, you may want to drive the first part of the canyon a few times to familiarize yourself with the terrain. The areas are listed in order starting at the mouth of the canyon and moving east. The individual approach descriptions will indicate which side of the canyon they are on.

There are several areas in the canyon that are closed to climbing. Be sure not to trespass and make matters worse. Instead, try and take productive measures to reopen these areas.

The Cantina
pg 63

I (5.3 C2)							
5.0-5.7	5.8	5.9	5.10	5.11	5.12	5.13	5.14

The Green Snatch
pg 66

I	I	I					
5.0-5.7	5.8	5.9	5.10	5.11	5.12	5.13	5.14

The Diamond
pg 68

I		2	2	I			
5.0-5.7	5.8	5.9	5.10	5.11	5.12	5.13	5.14

Nuts and Bolts
pg 70

	2	I	I				
5.0-5.7	5.8	5.9	5.10	5.11	5.12	5.13	5.14

The Ice Wall
pg 72

I		I	I	I	2	I	
A2	5.8	5.9	5.10	5.11	5.12	5.13	5.14

The Pipe Wall
pg 74

			I	I			
5.0-5.7	5.8	5.9	5.10	5.11	5.12	5.13	5.14

Area	5.0-5.7	5.8	5.9	5.10	5.11	5.12	5.13	5.14
5.8 Wall pg 78	1	3	1					
Utah Wall/Utah Gully pg 81	5	3			3	1		
Upper Utah Wall pg 84			1	3	1			
Roadside Attraction pg 87				1	2			
Chouinard's Crack Area pg 89	1		1					
Chouinard's Chimney Area pg 90	3							
Ruben and Ed Wall pg 92	3							
Moonlight Overhang Area pg 94	4							
Hole in the Rock pg 96	2	2	2	1				
The Blob pg 100				3	2			
Killer Crag Area pg 102				1	3	3	1	
The Cave pg 106	3 projects and 1 unknown route							
Indian Trail Limestone pg 108						2		

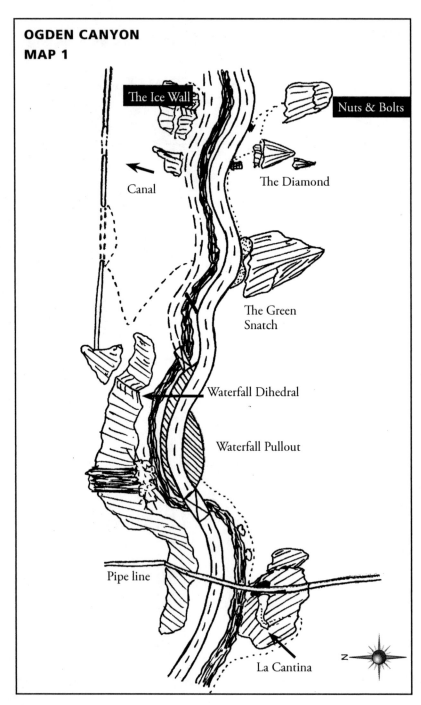

OGDEN CANYON
MAP 1

The Ice Wall

Nuts & Bolts

Canal

The Diamond

The Green
Snatch

Waterfall Dihedral

Waterfall Pullout

Pipe line

La Cantina

N

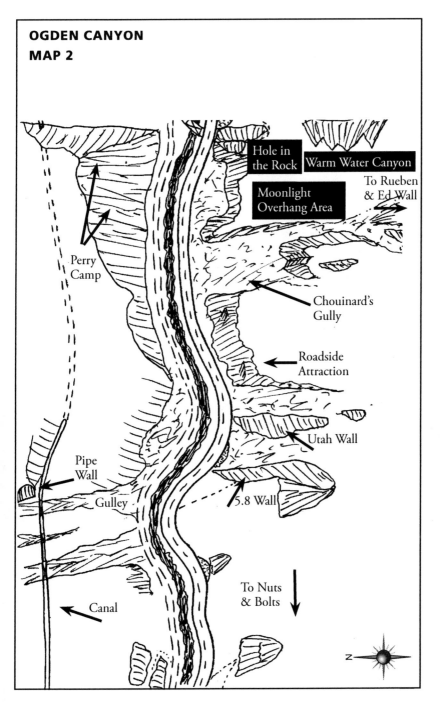

OGDEN CANYON
MAP 2

Hole in the Rock

Warm Water Canyon

To Rueben & Ed Wall

Moonlight Overhang Area

Perry Camp

Chouinard's Gully

Roadside Attraction

Utah Wall

Pipe Wall

Gulley

5.8 Wall

To Nuts & Bolts

Canal

N

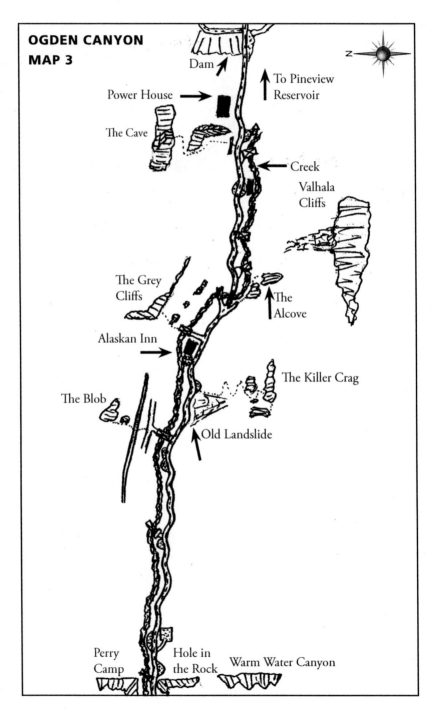

OGDEN CANYON
MAP 3

Dam

To Pineview
Reservoir

Power House

The Cave

Creek

Valhala
Cliffs

The Grey
Cliffs

The
Alcove

Alaskan Inn

The Killer Crag

The Blob

Old Landslide

Perry
Camp

Hole in
the Rock

Warm Water Canyon

LA CANTINA

La Cantina is the first route to come into sight on the right as you enter Ogden Canyon. This intimidating route remained unclimbed despite its striking appearance until 1998. Although the route remains an aid climb, it can and will go free. All but the last ten feet has been freed at 5.11. (Crag location reference on overview map pg 60).

Approach: Park at the waterfall pullout on the south side of the road. Take the trail at the west end of the pullout. Follow the trail as it traverses along the hillside above the river and past a few hot pots. Continue along the river a few yards past a large cave until you can go no further. The route is located on the overhanging corner directly over the river.

Descent: Scramble (fourth class) up and to the west until Rainbow Gardens can be seen. Then, angle west down a steep slope to the river. From here, either ford the river or continue downstream to cross the bridge at Rainbow Gardens.

___**A. La Cantina** 5.3 C2 ★
Free climb (5.3) up the right-angling ramp to the start of the dihedral. Aid climb up the dihedral to a small roof near the top. Move left around the roof and then scramble up the loose slope above (third class). Belay by slinging a horn on the upper slope.

WATERFALL DIHEDRAL (CLOSED TO CLIMBING)

This area is located directly east of the waterfall at the mouth of the canyon and straight across the river from the pullout. Climbers should be aware that these routes are rarely climbed and are known for loose rock and bad protection. More than one climber has had a close call here. Despite the reputation there are some routes worth climbing especially if your honing your aid skills. There is a two-bolt anchor on the belay ledge, but one of the bolts is bad. Unfortunately, the climbs are currently closed due to their close proximity to the waterfall. Watch out for poison ivy on the approach. (Crag location reference on overview map pg 60.)

___A. Unknown
This is the furthest left route on the wall. It has a few fixed pins and is most likely an old aid line.

___B. Lowe Route
This is an old aid line which was freed in a unique manner by Greg Lowe in the late 1960s. Unable to find reliable protection, but determined to climb the route anyway, he safely lead by first fixing a looped rope along side the crack. He then clipped each loop as he reached it just as a modern sport climber would clip bolts. The route's difficulty is unknown.

___C. Pecker Route A2+ ★
This is a more exciting variation to the *Regular Route*. Take a standard nailing rack, bird beaks, and a change of underwear.

___D. Regular Route A2
Although much of this route is fixed, a little creativity is needed to link things up. Beware of some of the fixed pins.

___E. Dihedral Corner 5.9+
The crack in the back of the main dihedral. Take some big gear for the upper section and watch for loose rock.

___F. Mr. Toad's Wild Ride
Named for the epic fall which nearly killed Bob Ellis and sent his belayer, Dave Black, to the hospital on the first ascent. The route climbs the face just left of the arête and is difficult to protect. The route's difficulty is unknown.

___G. Perkin's Folly 5.7 R
All that is known of this ambiguous route is that it climbs the broken face out right of the arête.

THE GREEN SNATCH

These rarely-climbed routes probably deserve more attention than they get. However, due to loose rock within close proximity of the road, extreme caution must be taken when climbing them. All belays must be built out of gear and helmets are advised. (Crag location reference on overview map pg 60).

Approach: Park at the pullout located on the righthand side of the road 0.2 mile up the canyon from the waterfall. The routes start directly above the pullout.

Descent: Rappel from a large pine tree on the top into a gully to the east. Then walk down the gully back to the base.

___A. Lyell's Variation 5.6

This is an alternate start to *The Green Snatch*. It begins in the corner above the east pullout and is more interesting than the regular start. It stays to the left side of the moss covered slabs for one pitch and then reconnects with *The Green Snatch* shortly into the second pitch.

___B. The Green Snatch 5.8

Take a standard free rack and a few extra runners.
Pitch 1: Start on the obvious moss-covered slabs between the two pullouts and climb up to a tree belay in the corner.
Pitch 2: Continue up the corner and then move left below the roof. Build an awkward belay just below the prominent 5.8 face with a nice hand crack.
Pitch 3: Climb the crack system up the center of the face to a tree belay on top.

___C. The Green Snatch Roof 5.10

Climb the first pitch of *The Green Snatch*, then traverse right from the middle of the second pitch. Belay on a small ledge directly below the obvious roof where a fixed pin can be seen on the face above. The final pitch pulls the roof and then follows the slot above to the top. This is a somewhat bold lead on questionable protection.

THE DIAMOND

The Diamond is a popular and fun area due to its short approach and moderate routes. It has several quality routes all of which are worth climbing. It is north-facing making it a good place for hot summer days. All routes, except *Bumbling Gumbies*, share the same anchors. (Crag location reference on overview map pg 68.)

Approach: Use the Green Snatch pullout located on the south side of the road 0.2 mile up the canyon from the waterfall. From the pullout, walk east 35 yards along the road until you reach an old, rock sign foundation. Take the short trail that cuts up the hillside just past this foundation. The Diamond is straight up the hill from the sign foundation. It is easily seen from the road and can be recognized by it's polished, triangular face.

___**A. Bumbling Gumbies** 5.10a ★
This three bolt sport route is located around the east side of The Diamond. It is a short, steep climb on good holds. No photo.

___**B. Lichen Life** 5.10a ★
This is the five bolt sport route on the far left side of The Diamond's main face. A good climb with sporty spaces between some of the bolts.

___**C. Blade Runner** 5.11c R/X ★
This bold line was first lead by the late Kent Jameson with natural gear and pitons long before the bolts on *Da Kine* were placed. The pitons have since been chopped, making it bolder still. It is virtually impossible to protect until it connects with *Da Kine* near the top.

___**D. Da Kine** 5.9 ★★
Fun sequences with good edging. This well-protected five-bolt sport route climbs straight up the center of The Diamond's polished face.

___**E. Diamond Direct** 5.9+ ★
A good gear route that is little tricky to protect. Take a set of nuts and small cams.

___**F. Diamond Spire** 5.6 (no photo)
This is the small spire located above The Diamond's main face. Approach by scrambling up and around the east side of The Diamond. The route begins on the east side of the spire and works its way around to the northwest. Belay on top using two old pitons that need backed up. Take a standard free rack and rappel off.

NUTS AND BOLTS

Another popular summertime crag with high quality routes. It has a short approach, abundant shade, and is north-facing. Most of the climbing requires at least some natural pro. (Crag location reference on overview map pg 60).

Approach: Use the Green Snatch pullout located on the south side of the road 0.2 mile up the canyon from the waterfall. Walk east along the road for 60 yards just past a group of trees and then take a trail angling southeast up the hillside. Hike through some trees to the base of the cliff. *Nuts and Bolts* is easily seen from the road.

A. Kitchen Pass 5.8

 Start in the corner alcove left of *Nuts and Bolts* and follow the right-angling cracks out of the corner up to a roof. Edge your way up the crack, angling left beneath the roof until the easy slabs above are gained. Build an anchor on top and walk off down the gully to the east. Protection is available, but it is often necessary to place it in questionable rock. If not for some loose rock, this would be a genial route. Take a standard free rack and some steady nerves.

B. Nuts and Bolts 5.8 ★★★

Climb to the first bolt of *No Nuts* before angling left over the small roof. Continue up the face aiming for the big slot in the roof above. Climb through the slot to your choice of bolted anchors either on the left or right. There is an easier variation which traverses left under the first roof and then straight up to the slot. The protection is there, but you'll have to hunt for it. Take a standard free rack.

C. No Nuts 5.10a ★★★

A great seven-bolt sport route to the right of *Nuts and Bolts*. This climb has a little of everything; friction, thin face climbing, and a jug haul over the second roof. Take a #2 or #2.5 Friend to protect the second roof if you need it. Bolted anchor.

D. Numb Nuts 5.9

Follow the left-facing dihedral to the right of *No Nuts* until it connects with *No Nuts* beneath the second roof. Watch for loose rock. A standard gear rack is needed.

THE ICE WALL

The Ice Wall gets its name from the multitude of ice climbs that used to form on it from leaks in the pipeline above. The leaks have long been fixed, but the name remains. Now it's host to a few good sport routes and one aid line. (Crag location reference on overview map pg 60).

Approach: Park at the waterfall pullout and cross the wooden bridge to the east. Hike east along the fisherman's path for 0.2 mile until the crag can be seen on the left. *Sesame Street* and *The Chopper* start right off the trail, but the other routes start off a ledge system above. The upper routes are gained by hiking up the steep slope around the east side of the cliff.

___A. Sesame Street 5.12a ★

A short three-bolt route that starts off the fisherman's trail. Don't let its name and appearance fool you. This is a steep difficult route which uses polished, down sloping ledges. A stick-clip is recommended for the first bolt.

___B. The Chopper A2

This short aid route is for the aid climber looking to get a quick fix. It climbs the ultra thin crack just to the right of Sesame Street and shares the same anchors. Take a small nailing rack with extra RURPs and beaks.

___**C. Aid Crisis** 5.13b

This is the sport route located to the right of *The Chopper*. You'll have to crimp, pinch, gaston, and mantel your way up this overhanging wall to reach the anchor. Unfortunately, this route was placed a little too close to *The Chopper* making it possible to clip some of the bolts while on the aid route. Five bolts.

___**D. Walk of the Wild Child**
5.12b/c ★

To access this route one must gain the upper ledge and then scramble around the corner to the west. Five bolts long with sustained climbing.

___**E. Decepticon** 5.11b★★

A difficult start followed by fun face climbing on thin edges. Beware of the high first clip. Four bolts.

___**F. Blues From a Gun** 5.10b★

More good face climbing with surprisingly involved sequences. An excellent warm-up for the other routes. Five bolts.

___**G. The Pull Zone** 5.9+++

This cruxy, seven-bolt route is easy 5.9 until the very top. Between the last bolt and the anchor is a horrendous boulder problem finish. The rating is unconfirmed. Good luck.

Mike Pleinis climbing on the Ice Wall—back when it actually formed ice

THE PIPE WALL

The Pipe Wall has two of the most exposed sport routes in the canyon. It over-hangs dramatically for its entire length and has excellent rock quality. There are currently only two routes but room for more exists. The wall is west-facing and is in the shade for much of the day. (Crag location reference on overview map pg 61).

Approach: Park at the waterfall pullout in the mouth of the canyon and cross the wooden bridge to the east. Follow the fisherman's trail east along the river for half a mile until you reach a telephone pole marked with a number 16. At this point, head left up a steep talus slope and into a gully where the pipeline can be seen spanning the gully above. When the pipeline is reached, the Pipe Wall will be visible on the right a little further up the gully. There is a short third class scramble to the start of the climbs. *Light at the End of the Tunnel* is not on the main wall (see the route description for more information).

Tim Nyugen on SesameStreet 5.12a   Photograph by David G. Robb

___A. Project

This route has yet to be redpointed, but when finished it will be an outstanding 5.12+ or 5.13-. Currently, there are only five bolts which make it a bit sporty going to the anchor. There is, however, a possibility that a sixth bolt will soon be added.

___B. Fill in the Blank 5.12b ★★

Fill in the Blank is named for the crux section which eluded the first ascensionist for a long time. This is a steep, high quality route well worth the hike. A stick-clip for the first bolt is recommended. Four bolts.

___C. Light at the End of the Tunnel
5.10 ★ (no photo)

A good warm-up for the other routes. This route, however, is not located on the Pipe Wall. If approaching from the Pipe Wall itself, simply walk west along the pipeline until the tunnel where the route is located is reached. If approaching from the waterfall pullout, take the fisherman's trail to the first telephone pole and then follow a utility road as it cuts up the hillside to the pipeline. Then, walk along the pipeline around the first tunnel and through the second. The route is at the end of the second tunnel. Four bolts.

STEPHAN SIEGRIST ON LA VIDA ES
SILBAR, ROTE FLUH (27 PITCH 5.12D)
EIGERNORDWAND, SWITZERLAND
PHOTO: THOMAS ULRICH

5.8 WALL

5.8 Wall is one of the most popular areas in the canyon due to an easy approach and high quality routes. All the routes can be toproped making this a great place for beginners. The routes here were first climbed as early as the 1950s. They were never named and have since become known simply by their location on the wall. In order to prevent access issues, do not park directly below the wall. Be responsible. There have been many complaints about climbers causing traffic hazards. Please follow the approach instructions below. (Crag location reference on overview map pg 61).

Approach: 5.8 Wall is located half a mile up the canyon from the waterfall. To approach it, park at the Hole in the Rock pullout located 0.8 mile up the canyon directly across the road from Perry Camp. Then, walk back down the canyon to the 5.8 Wall. Be sure to be careful and courteous of traffic while walking along the road. To toprope the wall, continue walking several yards down the canyon past the climbs until a trail cuts up the hill on the left to the top (see Upper 5.8 Wall photo).

___**A. Left III** 5.9+ R/X ★★

This bold route is basically a free solo if led. By the time there is any pro to be had the route is over. A good route with difficult friction climbing. Bolt anchor.

___**B. Left II** 5.8+ R ★★

Another bold lead with scarce protection and fun friction. Small cams, nuts, and micro-nuts are needed. Bolt anchor.

___**C. Left I** 5.8+ R ★★

Yet another runout and exciting lead. Take small cams, nuts and micro nuts. Bolt anchor.

___**D. Standard Crack** 5.7 ★★

This is a classic crack with great protection. A good route for beginning leaders. Anchor at the bolts.

___**E. Right I** 5.8 ★

The crack furthest to the right which then angles continuously to the left. The pro can be a little tricky. It shares an anchor with *Standard Crack*.

THE UPPER 5.8 WALL

The Upper 5.8 Wall is located above and southwest of the main wall. Approach by climbing one of the 5.8 Wall routes or by taking the trail a short distance down canyon from the main 5.8 Wall (see approach for 5.8 Wall). The Upper 5.8 Wall is just a short distance directly uphill from the top of 5.8 Wall. There are many possibilities for fun climbs, however, *Another Friend* is the only established route.

___F. Another Friend 5.7 ★★

This is the best, and only, recorded route on the Upper 5.8 Wall. Follow the meandering cracks just left of the main arête for two pitches. Bring some big cams besides a standard free rack. Watch for some loose rock on the second pitch. Descend east down the main gully until a ledge system traverses back to the base of the route.

80

UTAH WALL/UTAH GULLY

The Utah Wall and Upper Utah Wall have the most diverse climbing of any area in Ogden Canyon. There are classic traditional routes ranging from 5.5 to 5.10 alongside quality sport routes. This area should not be missed. (Crag location reference on overview map pg 61.)

Approach: The Utah Wall is located 0.6 mile up the canyon from the waterfall. Park at the Hole in the Rock pullout which is located 0.8 mile up the canyon from the waterfall, then hike back down the canyon to the Utah Wall. It is in the second major gully on the south side of the road. Follow the steep loose trail up the west side of the gully next to the wall. Be extremely careful not to knock rocks into the road!

___**A. I Love My Wife, But She Doesn't Climb** 5.7 ★
Climb the broken and dirty crack for 100 feet. A fun climb that will get better with subsequent ascents. Take a standard free rack. Belay must be built on top.

___**B. Unnamed** 5.8+
This is the thin crack to the right of A. When the crack dies out, face climb up to the small roof. Skirt the roof on the left (easy) or pull straight over it (5.9). The original route then crosses the dihedral and finishes on the face to the left. This way is loose and not recommended. Instead, finish in the dihedral or on the face to the right of the arête. Take a standard free rack and some TCUs. The belay must be built on top.

___**C. Unnamed Dihedral** 5.5 or 5.6?
This is the obvious dirty dihedral to the left of *Utah Crack*. The rating, although certainly easy, is unconfirmed. Belays must be built.

___**D. Utah Crack** 5.5 ★★
This is the prominent, two-pitch crack in the center of the wall. The first pitch is the best and is nearly 100 feet long. It ends at a bolt belay. Pitch two takes you to the top of the cliff. The belay must be built on top. Take a standard free rack. Walk off to the south.

___**E. In the Pink** 5.8 ★★
This route pulls the far left end of the roof. Take some natural pro for the bottom section. Two bolts protect the face above the roof. It has a bolt belay.

81

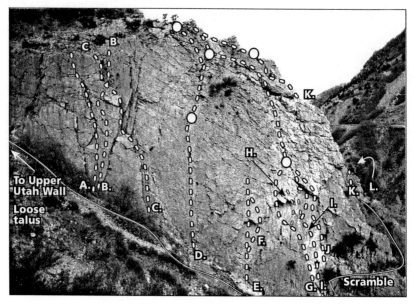

A. I Love My Wife... 5.7
B. Unnamed 5.8+
C. Unnamed Dihedral 5.5 or 5.6?
D. Utah Crack 5.5
E. In the Pink 5.8
F. Sink the Pink 5.11

G. Apex 5.7
H. Apex Right 5.8
I. Shotgun 5.6
J. Lawyers, Guns, and Money 5.10b
K. Air Time 5.10c
L. M-37 5.10-

___F. Sink the Pink 5.11 TR ★

A toprope variation to *In the Pink*. It climbs the overhang to the right of the main route.

___G. Apex 5.7 ★

Start by following the left-angling ledge left of *Shotgun*. Pull the roof where it forms a corner and climb the face above to the anchor for *Shotgun*. It should be noted that the original route actually angled up and left to eventually connect with *Utah Crack* rather than *Shotgun*. This was long before the bolts were placed on *In the Pink*.

___H. Apex Right 5.8

This is a variation which climbs straight over the roof to the right of *Apex*.

___I. Shotgun 5.6 ★★★

A classic route which follows an excellent splitter crack. Climb the obvious crack system into the highest corner of the overhang, step out of the roof, and then ascend the face above to the belay. A harder variation pulls the overhang lower down (5.9). A great climb not to be missed. Take a standard free rack.

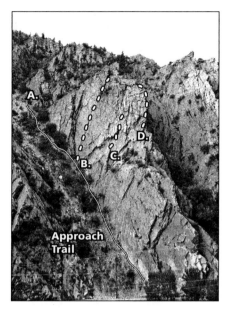

A. Upper Utah Wall
D. Utah Crack
I. Shot Gun
K. Air Time

___J. Lawyers, Guns, and Money
5.10b ★
This climb has the notoriety of being the first rap-bolted route in Ogden. It gets its name from the controversy it caused with the local traditionalists due to its close proximity to *Shotgun*. It follows five bolts up a polished face. At the top of the face, climb the hand crack over the roof right of *Shotgun*. Continue up the face above to the anchor for *Shotgun*. A light natural pro rack is needed to protect the upper half of the climb.

___K. Air Time 5.10c ★★★
A definite classic and one of the best routes in the canyon. It climbs the exposed north arête of the wall. To reach its base, scramble up and right of *Shotgun* to the edge of the arête. Start the route by climbing the east face up to a fixed pin. Move to the right out onto the arête and up an awkward ramp to a splitter crack in a corner. At the top of the splitter is a good ledge where the route splits. The original route moves left onto the east face and up to the belay. The *Hadley Variation* continues to follow the main crack system angling right of the arête. Both ways are well worth doing. The anchor on top must be built. Descend by rappelling off a horn down *Shotgun* or do one more easy pitch and walk off. Take a standard free rack.

___L. M-37 5.10- ★★ (no photo)
This route is named after a military issue 1953 Dodge Power Wagon. Start in the same place as *Air Time* and climb the crack system to the right around on the underside of the arête. The route runs parallel to *Air Time* about ten or fifteen feet away. The anchor and descent are the same as for *Air Time*. Take a standard free rack.

UPPER UTAH WALL

The Upper Utah Wall has very little in common with the lower Utah Wall. It has short, vertical, and relatively difficult routes as compared with the long, low-angle routes on the Utah Wall. There is a mixture of sport and trad climbing. Originally, the sport routes here were a bold, exciting mixture of bolts and natural pro, but in 2001 someone retro bolted them. Now only *Bangkok* requires anything more than quick draws. This is unethical and narrow minded. Please do not alter already existing routes. Respect the traditional ethic of the first ascensionist (see Ethics section). Most of the routes can be toproped by hiking around the left side, but you might have to anchor off a few trees and/or some natural pro to reach the bolt anchors. (Crag location reference on overview map pg 61).

Approach: Follow the approach description for the lower Utah Wall (pg 81). Once in the gully, continue up the steep scree past the Utah Wall until the Upper Utah Wall comes into view on the right. It is recognized as a much smaller cliff detached from the main wall (see Utah Wall Overview).

___A. Astronomy 5.10c/d ★
The far left route on the wall.

___B. 911 5.11a ★★
Thin edges and fun sidepulls angle continuously left. Two buttonhead bolts and two pitons of questionable integrity used to make this lead exciting. That's why it was named 911. It shares the final bolt and the anchor with *Astronomy*. Four bolts.

___C. Bangkok 5.10b/c ★★★
Three bolts of good, fun, thin edging followed by jugs to the top. The space between the second and third bolt is a little runout, but a small TCU will protect it. This route makes the hike up the death scree worth it.

___D. Buckets for Bucky 5.9 ★★
This is a worthy crack climb that will take some creativity to protect. Bring a standard free rack. Shares an anchor with *Syd Barret's Corner*.

___E. Syd Barret's Corner 5.10a ★★
A must-do for Pink Floyd fans. This often-ignored climb is well worth the time and quite fun. The original route begins below the main ledge where the other routes start from (start not shown in photo). You can also start off the main ledge and bypass the first two bolts. Three bolts protect the start, but natural pro is needed for the rest.

Ogden Canyon Waterfall   Photograph by David G. Robb

ROADSIDE ATTRACTION

These seldom-climbed routes serve as a proving ground for advanced trad climbers. You haven't "come of age" until you've climbed *Roadside Attraction*. The area is great for hot summertime days since it's close to the river, the approach is short, and it rarely gets any sun. (Crag location reference on overview map pg 61).

Approach: The area is located 0.6 mile up the canyon from the waterfall. Park at the Hole in the Rock pullout 0.8 mile from the waterfall and then walk back down the canyon to the area. The climbs start right off the road on the east side of the mouth of the Utah Wall gully. This is the second major gully you will pass on the south side while walking down the road. It is easiest to belay from the road and not the top of the ramp. All routes share a bolt belay.

___A. Roadside Attraction
5.11a ★★★
An Ogden Canyon classic first put up by the late Kurt Stoddard. It stands as one of his most significant contributions to Ogden climbing before his untimely death. This is the steep, overhanging crack in the lefthand corner at the top of the approach ramp. Take a standard free rack and enjoy.

___B. Roadside Middle 5.11d ★★
This is the hard bold line that follows the pitons up the center of the overhang. The pitons are of marginal quality and should be backed up with natural pro when possible. Take small nuts and a few small cams. A great route for a competent leader.

___ C. Schweppe's Swing 5.10a ★★
This excellent route makes a good warm-up for the other two. Begin by following the right-angling ramp on the right side of the overhang. About halfway up, move into another crack system on the left. Take a standard free rack.

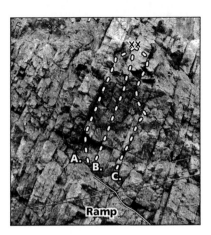

CHOUINARD'S GULLY

Chouinard's Gully boasts what is probably the best fist crack in the canyon as well as Ogden's only offwidth. Apparently, Yvon Chouinard climbed some of the routes in this area while visiting Ogden to give a climbing clinic. The routes here are spread out in the steep, loose, and confusing gully. Be aware that it may take some time to locate them because there are no real trails. (Crag location reference on overview map pg 61).

Approach: Chouinard's Gully is located 0.7 mile from the waterfall. To reach it, park at the Hole in the Rock pullout 0.8 mile from the waterfall and walk back down the canyon. It is the first major gully on the south side of the road. Each area has an individual approach description.

CHOUINARD'S GULLY OVERVIEW

To Ruben & Ed Wall

Diagonal Crack

Chouinard's Chimney

Chouinard's Crack

Moonlight Overhang

CHOUINARD'S CRACK AREA

Approach: This area can be easily identified from the road as the prominent dihedral in the center of the gully. To reach it, simply hike up the talus aiming straight at the big open book. Near the base of the routes some dangerous, grass-covered fourth class must be negotiated to reach a piton belay. (Crag location reference on overview map pg 61).

___**A. Chouinard's Crack** 5.9+ ★★★
This is the best fists and off-fists climbing in the canyon. Take #1 through #4 Camalots and don't bother with anything smaller. There is a chockstone that can be slung about half way up if you're short on big gear. Belay on top where you can sling some boulders.

___**B. Dirty Corner** 5.5
This is the crack in the corner to the right of *Chouinard's*. The name says it all.

89

CHOUINARD'S CHIMNEY AREA

Approach: Hike up the talus in the bottom of the main gully to the left of the open book where Chouinard's Crack is located. Continue up the gully a short distance above Chouinard's Crack until a prominent, east-facing cliff rises up on the right. Chouinard's Chimney is the obvious, gaping black offwidth near the north end of the cliffband. You must scramble up some ledges to reach the base. Diagonal Crack has its own approach information. (Crag location reference on overview map pg 61).

___A. Chouinard's Chimney 5.6 ★
This is a very misleading route name because it's not a chimney, it's an offwidth. However, no offwidth technique is required to climb it since the crack can be easily lie-backed or face climbed. There is a chockstone halfway up and a confident climber could lead the short route using only this. Otherwise, Big Bros are the only gear big enough to protect it. The route is also easily toproped by scrambling around the right side. The anchor on top requires mid-sized cams.

___B. Psychic Arête
Nothing is known of this route other than it climbs the outside arête right of *Chouinard's Chimney*.

___C. Unknown 5.7
Another little known route. It begins in the cracks just left of the arête above Chouinard's Chimney and then follows the arête.

___D. Diagonal Crack 5.7 ★★

The best approach for this route is
to simply climb *Chouinard's Crack* and
then scramble up and right into a small
chasm with a big pine tree where *Diagonal
Crack* starts. Otherwise, approach as for
Chouinard's Chimney and then scramble up
the ledges right of the chimney to the
top of the ridge. The east-facing route
comes into view at the top of the ridge,
but you must down-climb into the chasm
for the start. This is a somewhat comical
route because in 60 feet of climbing
you never get more than 25 feet off the
ground. Definitely a fun climb unlike any
other. Take nuts and small cams. Belay on
top and walk off.

RUBEN AND ED WALL

The routes here follow discontinuous cracks that are often hard to protect. There are many variations possible due to the fractured nature of the low-angle wall. Clean gear or small trees and long slings provide the anchor. (Crag location reference on overview map pg 61).

Approach: Approach as for *Chouinard's Chimney*, then continue on up the main gully past the chimney. When the gully splits, take the right fork and the wall will come into view shortly. It is recognized as a low-angle, east-facing cliffband on the right side of the gully. It's a long haul up the loose scree, but it's worth checking out. Descend all routes by walking off to the north.

___A. The Organization 5.6

Not the most aesthetic route, but since you just hiked all the way up here, you may as well climb it. Take a standard free rack.

___B. King of the Echo People

5.7★★

This is the best route on the wall. It consists of fun climbing on meandering cracks up the center of the wall. Take a standard free rack.

___C. Andy Warhol Sucks a Big One

5.7 ★

This route starts on the right of the arch, traverses to the roof, and then exits the nice hand crack on the left. The first half of the route is the most fun and makes up for the loose rock and shrubs above. Take a standard free rack.

Mad Squad Member Crista Hollenberg   Photo by JM Casanova

Crista's passion is climbing
Our passion is friction.
www.madrockclimbing.com

MOONLIGHT OVERHANG AREA

This small area is nice because it is very accessible without being right on the road. It also contains one of the few chimney routes in the canyon. (Crag location reference on overview map pg 61).

Approach: Park at the Hole in the Rock pullout located 0.8 mile up the canyon from the waterfall. Walk a few yards down the canyon around the north face of Hole in the Rock. The *Bird's Perch* and *Chimney* are located in a corner on the left at the west end of the tunnel for which Hole in the Rock is named. *Moonlight Overhang* is at the southwest end of this same alcove a little further down the canyon.

___**A. The Bird's Perch** 5.7
This vague route starts at the base of the chimney, but climbs the face to the left. Take a standard free rack. Descend down a gully to the southeast which leads to the base of Hole in the Rock.

___**B. Chimney** 5.7
A dirty chimney with a few fun moves. The left variation has the best climbing with a nice hand crack in the back of the chimney, but is slightly harder. Take a standard free rack. Descend as for *The Bird's Perch*.

___C. Moonlight Overhang 5.7 ★

This is an excellent, though short, route that presents a great alternative to *Hole in the Rock*. There are three variations all worth climbing. The regular route climbs the seam in the face directly beneath the left corner of the overhang. This way provides the best climbing, but it is a little hard to protect until the roof is reached. When you reach the roof you can pull over the corner (5.8) or traverse right (5.7). Take a small free rack. Belay on a small tree and rappel off.

___D. Moonshadow Variation 5.6

A better protected variation to *Moonlight Overhang*. It begins in the corner to the right. Take a small free rack. Belay on a small tree and rappel off.

HOLE IN THE ROCK

Hole in the Rock is the most accessible cliff in the canyon. The approach consists of simply getting exiting your car. Consequently, it is also one of the most popular areas in the canyon even though the route quality is marginal. Its distinguishing characteristics include an annoying cable which traverses the entire cliff and a hole blasted through the rock for a pipeline. All routes can be toproped by scrambling up the steep gully on the left side of the cliff. (Crag location reference on overview map pgs 61, 62).

Approach: Drive 0.8 mile up the canyon from the waterfall and park in the pullout directly below the cliff on the south side of the road. It is across the street from Perry Camp.

___A. Chicken Wire 5.8 ★

The three-bolt sport route to the right of the hole. It consists of intricate smearing between good holds. The first few feet is probably the hardest. The first bolt is quite high which leaves the cable as the only option for protection right off the deck (hence the name). The spaces between the other bolts are a bit sporty. It shares an anchor with *Hole in the Rock*.

___B. Hole in the Rock 5.5 ★

A great route for the beginning trad leader, as well as a great toprope for novice climbers. This is the obvious crack starting out of the hole. It would have received two stars were it not for the cable. Take a standard free rack. Bolt belay.

___C. Twinkle Toes 5.9+ R

A very bold lead with the cable as the only substantial gear. There are several variations possible.

___D. Layback Crack 5.6 ★

This is the righthand crack on the main face. Another fun climb, but a little harder to protect than *Hole in the Rock*. You'll need a standard free rack.

___E. Outer Rim 5.9+ R ★

The very dangerous direct start of this route actually begins from the road around the righthand side of the main face. It climbs the various fragile cracks directly over the road and is not recommended. The better alternative is to start from the ledge above the main Hole in the Rock Wall where routes F and G begin. Climb the runout face between the two bolted lines. There are only two or three gear placements in the fifty feet of climbing on the upper face. The real challenge is to resist traversing to one side or the other to clip a bolt.

For the original start, take a standard free rack with a few TCUs. For the upper face just bring a set of nuts and a handful of TCUs. Shares an anchor with routes F and G.

Note: *Routes F and G begin on the ledge above and slightly right of the main face and share an anchor with E. Reach them by climbing up the gully to the left of the main Hole in the Rock wall (or just climb one of the routes on the main wall). Then traverse to the right (north) out on a narrow, scary ledge to a belay anchor located directly over the road. Be extremely careful not to knock rocks onto cars below.*

___F. If the Fall Doesn't Kill You, A Car Will 5.10 ★★

The footwork on this one will make you think. Thin edging and crimps between spaced-out good holds. Height dependent moves make it a little harder for short people. There is a big, loose flake to the left of the route about half way up. Do not touch it! If it fell, it would likely kill your belayer and then land in the road. Six bolts.

___G. Sudden Exposure 5.8 ★★

This is an exciting and aptly named route. Traverse straight right from the belay and follow four bolts up the arête. Bring clean gear for the last twenty feet or you'll be in for a long runout.

PERRY CAMP AND WARM WATER CANYON (CLOSED TO CLIMBING)

Perry Camp and Warm Water Canyon contain what is some of the best climbing in Ogden Canyon. They are located 0.8 mile up Ogden Canyon from the waterfall. Warm Water Canyon is the gully on the south side of the road above Hole in the Rock. Perry Camp is on the north side of the road across the river. Unfortunately, these areas are on private land and are currently closed to climbing. In the past there have been rumors that the rock itself is not on private land and that only the approach is considered trespassing. This is not true. All of Warm Water Canyon and both the south and east faces of Perry Camp are privately owned. Do not trespass. You will only make it more likely that the areas will remain closed forever. If you want to climb in these areas, then work with the land owners to gain their trust. Write kind, well thought out letters. Organize other climbers. Join the Access Fund. Do not make the situation worse by sneaking onto other people's property. Be constructive. (Crag location reference on overview map pg 62).

WARM WATER CANYON

The Rib   The Coffin   The Shovels

PERRY CAMP EAST FACE

PERRY CAMP SOUTH FACE

THE BLOB

If you want to climb some quality limestone sport routes of a moderate grade, go to Logan Canyon. If you can't go to Logan Canyon, then you'll have to settle for The Blob. This area and the Killer crag are the only well-developed limestone crags in Ogden Canyon. The rock here is a little loose and flaky, but will probably get better with subsequent ascents. It's a place every Ogden climber should try once, but you might not go back. (Crag location reference on overview map pg 62).

Approach: When approaching this area be extremely quiet and courteous of the local homeowners. Park in a gravel pullout on the north side of the road two miles upcanyon from the waterfall. This pullout is just a few dozen yards from a bridge spanning the river. Do not drive across the bridge. Walk across the bridge and continue north to where the road makes a T. Straight ahead and behind a dumpster a trail angles to the right up a steep scree slope. Take this trail up to the pipeline and walk east along the cement until you reach a manhole. A short distance past the manhole, the trail climbs steeply into the trees on the left. It is usually overgrown, but by aiming straight uphill past a few small cliffs, The Blob can be reached in about fifteen minutes. Plan on bushwhacking and steep hiking.

___**A. Frankenclimb** 5.10c ★

Rightly named. Fun, yet bizarre climbing for five bolts. This is the only route on the west face. It starts behind the big boulder at the southwest corner of the cliff and follows a corner system to a small roof. Pull the roof and gain a ledge with anchors. This is the best route on The Blob.

___**B. The Fly** 5.11a

Thin face climbing on flaky rock. It's a little runout to the last bolt. Watch for loose rock near the top. Six bolts.

___**C. Paper Cut** 5.11c

This is a toprope variation to *The Fly*. Cut left at the second bolt and then straight up to the anchors. Sharp, thin face climbing on flaky rock.

___**D. The Fury** 5.10a

The crux is getting past the first bolt on thin edges. Then it's fun face climbing to the top. The second best route on the wall. Three bolts.

___**E. Attack of the Twenty Foot Climb** 5.10b

A very fun and very short climb using some big pockets. Two bolts.

KILLER CRAG AREA

The Killer Crag is a lonely limestone sport climbing area located high on the south side of the canyon in the shade of a thick pine grove. Unlike most of the limestone in Ogden Canyon, the rock here is of good quality and the approach is tolerable. The area is a great alternative to the crowds at 9th Street or the poor rock of The Blob. Most of the route names here have a story behind them, but, trust me, you don't want to know them. The route difficulty ranges from 5.10 to 5.13 and varies in length from 35 to 70 feet.

In addition to the Killer Crag, there are three other areas in the vicinity with existing routes: The Inner Struggle Wall, Yoda Cave and The Tower. Expect to see more development in this area as climbers discover more crags hidden in the thick pine forests. (Crag location reference on overview map pg 62).

Approach: Park at a pullout on the south side of the road just before the Alaskan Inn, 2.3 miles upcanyon from the waterfall. Walk west down the road for approximately 50 yards to a faint trail rising steeply up the grassy hillside. This trail is vague at best, so plan on spending a little time finding your way around. The trail soon turns rocky and steep, but only for a short distance before cutting left into the trees. Be sure not to miss this turn or you will be sucked straight up into the extremely loose and steep scree. At this point the trail becomes easier to see. It turns steep briefly before beginning to switchback its way up the hillside. After the third switchback, while angling west, the Inner Struggle Wall will become visible through the trees on the left. Just past the Inner Struggle Wall, the trail turns steep again before continuing to angle west. When the trail again switches back east, Yoda Cave is seen 20 yards off the trail to the west. Four more switchbacks later and you're at the Central Killer Crag.

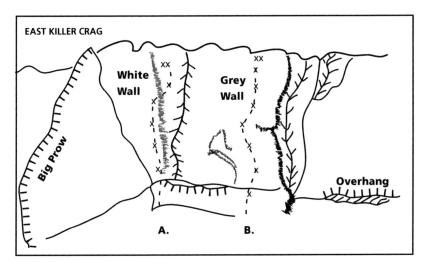

EAST KILLER CRAG

___**A. Dick Spic** 5.12c ★★

Crimpy and technical climbing. Be sure not to clip the anchor too soon and miss out on the exhilarating final dyno to a bomber hold above and right of the anchor. Five bolts.

___**B. Grifter** 5.10d ★★

Fun continuous face climbing on crimps and smears. The first bolt is a little on the high side. The crux is between the fourth and sixth bolts. Seven bolts.

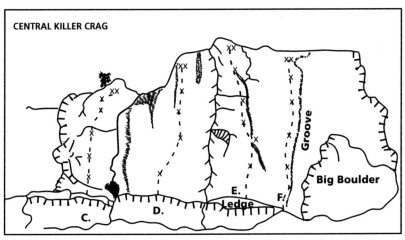

Descriptions on following page.

C. Domer

D. Blue Mask 5.12b

E. Munge 5.13a

F. Shocker 5.11c

CENTRAL KILLER CRAG

___C. Domer (project)

This striking project was named for the serial killer Jeffery Domer. This is how the Killer Crag gets its name. Five bolts.

___D. Blue Mask 5.12b ★

Awkward climbing up a mottled, cheese-grater face to a short slab. Loose to the second bolt. A stick-clip is recommended. Four bolts.

___E. Munge 5.13a

This is the hardest route in the area so far. The crux is on the lower half after which the climbing gets easier. The route angles strangely to the second bolt. A stick-clip is recommended. Five bolts.

___F. Shocker 5.11c ★

The crux is between the first and third bolts. Follow the crack to the top. Five bolts.

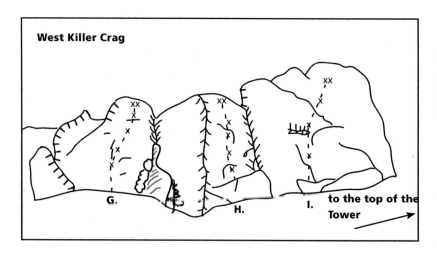

West Killer Crag

G.   H.   I.   to the top of the Tower

WEST KILLER CRAG

___G. Steamer 5.11b ★

Technical climbing up a clean gray face. Five bolts.

___H. Scared Boy 5.12a ★★★

A Killer Crag classic serving up a good healthy dose of sidepulls and liebacks on great rock. It takes an intuitive leader to pull off the crux between the third and fourth bolts. Four bolts.

___I. Sweet Tart 5.11d ★

Climb an engaging variety of slopers, cracks, pockets, and crimps in just 35 feet. Three bolts.

THE CAVE

The Cave is one of the most impressive rock formations in Ogden Canyon. At the deepest point, this 100-foot tall cliff overhangs an unbelievable 60 feet. Twenty-five of those feet are perfectly horizontal. This imposing cave has inspired four routes so far, but only one has been completed. The other three have been abandoned and still await stronger climbers to complete them. There is room for over a dozen routes to go up. Part of The Cave seeps in the spring making fall the best time of year to climb. The rock quality varies from poor to marginal. This means extensive cleaning is necessary for new routes. Strong and motivated climbers are greatly encouraged to go take a look. It might also be noted that there is a wide ledge system along the base that makes for a pleasant place to hang out. (Crag location reference on overview map pg 62.)

Approach: To view The Cave, drive a little more than four miles up the canyon to the water plant just below Pine View Dam. It sits high on the north side of the canyon and can't be missed. Do not hike directly up to The Cave from this point because of trespassing. Instead, park in a small pullout next to a utility shed on the south side of the road exactly four miles up the canyon from the waterfall. The Cave will not be visible from this point. Cross the street and walk east a short distance along an old unused road which leads behind a house. Hike straight up the mountainside aiming for a notch between the rocky ridge on the right and a cliff on the left. Once above the notch, traverse east until The Cave comes into view and then hike straight up. There is no real trail and some bush-whacking will be required. Approach time is about 45 minutes.

___A. Abandon Ship (project)

This less ambitious, and therefore, more reasonable route is left of the main overhang. It will probably be the easiest of the existing projects if it is ever completed (5.13?).

___B. Project

The bolts on this optimistic line ascend an upside down staircase which is nearly featureless.

___C. Project

This project takes the cake. It begins in the very back of the cave and aims straight over the center of the roof. The only way this route will ever be climbed is with a pair of aiders. Take that as a challenge if you want to.

___D. Unknown 5.11?

Dirty, loose, pitiful climbing. This is, however, the only completed route on the wall.

INDIAN TRAIL LIMESTONE

The Indian Trail Limestone is the beautiful looking buttress just south of the mouth of Ogden Canyon. It faces west so it gets morning shade and afternoon sun. Currently only two sport routes exist, but it's worth the hike to give them a try. The possibility for more routes exists both on the main buttress and on the surrounding rock. The Lowes climbed some of the crack systems in the area in the 60s and 70s, but little else is known. (Crag location reference on overview map pg 62).

Approach: Park at the 22nd Street parking lot for the Indian Trail trailhead. This is located at the eastern end of 22nd Street in Ogden where the road dead ends at the mountainside. There is a map at the trailhead to help anyone unfamiliar with the Indian Trail. Follow the Indian Trail up to the Hidden Valley cut off. Take the Hidden Valley trail for 150 yards to where a faint trail cuts straight up the mountainside at the beginning of a small meadow. Take the faint trail up to an old mine shaft. From this point the trail all but disappears. Hike around the right side of the shaft and straight up the mountainside until you are almost level with the main crag. From this point, traverse north to the crag. Some bushwhacking is unavoidable.

___**A. Well of Souls** 5.12a ★★
This route is located on the north end of the cliffband. Do a short face climb up to a ledge. Then climb a steep face through three big huecos to a slab. Fun stuff. Seven bolts.

___**B. Project**

___**C. Dances With Rock** 5.12b ★
Climb a clean, steep face up to a slab. Worth doing. Five bolts.

SCHOOLROOM WALL AREA

The Schoolroom Wall is the long, west-facing cliffband stretching from 22nd Street on the north to Taylor's Canyon on the south. Numerous routes of excellent quality reside along this quartzite bluff, but the view alone makes it worth the hike up the talus.

Very little information has survived on the routes done in this area prior to the mid-80s. During a recent revival of interest in this area, climbers often found relics from prior ascents on routes they thought had never been climbed. Due to this lack of information, there may be discrepancies in route names and ratings.

The wall has been divided into four sections: Asbury Park, BNF Area, Central Schoolroom, Tree Crack Area, and Taylor's Corner. Each section has an individual approach description.

There is a wide ledge system which traverses the entire cliffband known as the 4x4 Ledge. Most of the routes start off of this ledge. It should be noted that there is a natural break in the 4x4 Ledge that cuts off Asbury Park from the other sections of the wall. This break is located just a few yards south of *Father Roy*. It is not impassable, but it does require that some scary fourth class be climbed. Otherwise, the 4x4 Ledge can be easily traversed for the entire length of the Schoolroom Wall.

SCHOOLROOM WALL AREA

Ramp Routes
pg 112

5.0-5.7	5.8	5.9	5.10	5.11	5.12	5.13	5.14
I		4	4				

Asbury Park
pg 114

5.0-5.7	5.8	5.9	5.10	5.11	5.12	5.13	5.14
I	I		4	6	4	I	

BNF Area
pg 117

5.0-5.7	5.8	5.9	5.10	5.11	5.12	5.13	5.14
	I			2	I	I	

Central Scoolroom
pg 120

5.0-5.7	5.8	5.9	5.10	5.11	5.12	5.13	5.14
I		I	I	I			

The Tangerine
pg 124

5.0-5.7	5.8	5.9	5.10	5.11	5.12	5.13	5.14
			I	3			

5.10 Slab
pg 127

5.0-5.7	5.8	5.9	5.10	5.11	5.12	5.13	5.14
			4				

Tree Crack Area
pg 128

5.0-5.7	5.8	5.9	5.10	5.11	5.12	5.13	5.14
2	I	4	8	5	7		

Utahnics Wall
pg 134

5.0-5.7	5.8	5.9	5.10	5.11	5.12	5.13	5.14
I	2	I	I		I		

Taylor's Corner Area
pg 136

5.0-5.7	5.8	5.9	5.10	5.11	5.12	5.13	5.14
	3		I				

THE RAMP ROUTES AND ASBURY PARK

Asbury Park is located on the large prow at the north end of the School-room Wall.

Approach: Park at the Indian Trail parking lot located at the top (east end) of 22nd Street. Follow assorted meandering trails east up the hillside to where the 4x4 Ledge angles into the ground. This ledge is easily identified as the large grassy ramp that splits the Schoolroom cliffband in half. Hike south up the 4x4 Ledge until the routes come into view at the "prow" of the cliffband. You will pass the Ramp Routes halfway to the prow. Asbury Park can also be reached by hiking straight up the scree below the prow and then climbing the unnamed dihedral (route U on the Asbury Park Area photo) to the right of UP & L.

SCHOOLROOM NORTH APPROACH

RAMP ROUTES

___**A. Homecoming Princess** 5.9 ★★
Five bolts.

___**B. Blue Steel** 5.9 ★★
Runout to the anchor. Four bolts.

___**C. Interstellar** 5.9 ★★
Pull a big roof with a jug on the lip.
Sustained face climbing leads to the
anchors from the roof. Five bolts.

___**D. Phantasmagorical**
5.7 or 5.9 ★★★
Shares the first bolt with *Interstellar*.
There are two options at the second
bolt. The left is 5.9 and the right is 5.7.
Finish on the arête. Four bolts.

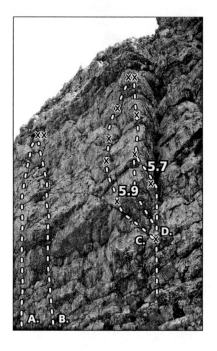

Routes E -H are located on a polished face split by a small overhang 100 feet uphill (south) of *Phantasmigorical.*

___**E.Catharsis** 5.9 ★★

Climb a slightly runout face up to the left side of the overhang. Then follow hidden buckets and a thin crack that angle continuously left up the steep, polished face. Take extra TCUs and a standard free rack. The anchor must be built on top. Descend by rappelling off the anchors for *FDR*.

___**F. Alienation Effect** 5.10 ★★

This bold first ascent was onsighted from the ground up with only one wobbly cam stuffed under the roof. Start as for *Catharsis*, but at the roof angle slightly right and then straight up. This steep and desperate face is difficult to protect, but it offers excellent climbing for the competent leader. Take extra

TCUs, a standard free rack and some steady nerves. The anchor must be built. Descend by rappelling off the anchors for *FDR*.

___**G. FDR** 5.10 ★★

A fun crack that pulls the right side of the overhang. Take a standard free rack. Bolt anchors.

___**H. Dork Crack** 5.5

This somewhat comical route follows the fun and easy flakes that angle to the right from the start of FDR. There is no need for an anchor because the route arcs right back to the ground.

113

ASBURY PARK

___A. Detroit Muscle (project)
Four-bolt sport route that pulls a big roof. A little rotten.

___B. Bound For Glory 5.12b ★★★
Excellent. Combines strength and finesse. Seven bolts.

___C. Badlands 5.12a ★★
5.10 climbing leads to a short crux just below the roof. Move left below the roof and exit on the arête. Six bolts.

___D. E Street 5.10c ★★
This is the crack in the back of the corner. Good, creative climbing that requires a variety of techniques. Take a standard free rack.

___E. Suicide Rap (project)
Five-bolt sport route on the face to the left of *E Street*.

___F. Rule of Three 5.13b ★★
Six bolt sport route that shares the start of *Suicide Rap*.

___G. Thunder Road 5.11d ★★
A high quality crack climb that pulls over a steep bulge. Take a standard free rack and a few extra small TCUs.

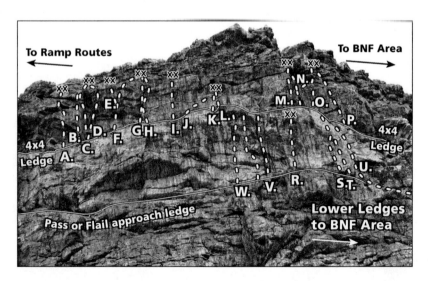

___**H. Jungleland** 5.12a ★★

Start to the right of *Thunder Road*. Near the third bolt, traverse left into the *Thunder Road* crack for a few moves to avoid some poor rock. Then move back right out onto the face and pull the final roof. Shares the anchor with *Thunder Road*. Six bolts.

___**I. Tenth Avenue (project)**

The thin crack located between *Jungleland* and *Flamingo Lane*.

___**J. Flamingo Lane** 5.8

The diagonal crack that leads to the anchors for *Pocket Loverboy*. Take a standard free rack.

___**K. Pocket Loverboy** 5.11c ★

Four bolts.

___**L. Stomach You Fears** 5.10b ★

This sport route makes a good warm up. It gets progressively harder as it goes. Shares the anchor with *Pocket Loverboy*. Four bolts.

Note: *Routes M through P start off of a big ledge at the base of A Country Mile. There is a belay bolt and a fixed pin on the ledge. Reach it by climbing some easy fifth class up to either the right or left sides of the ledge.*

___**M. Teardrops on the City** 5.11b ★★★

This one is a must-do. Five bolts of exposed climbing up the arête left of *A Country Mile*.

___**N. A Country Mile** 5.10 ★

AKA *Lunar Tune*. Stem your way up the thin crack inthe corner to a roof. Pull the roof on theleft and finishon *Teardrops on the City*. An easier variation (5.9) traverses right below the roof and shares an anchor with *Giants of Science*. The traverse is a little difficult to protect. Take a standard free rack.

___**O. Giants of Science** 5.11b ★★★

Excellent consistent climbing up perfect rock on the face right of *A Country Mile*. Six bolts.

___**P. Father Roy** 5.10d ★

Although this route is a little cruxy, it's well worth doing. Climb a hand crack over a bulge using an exhausting combination of jams, face holds, and liebacks. The climbing gets easier after the bulge, but watch for loose rock near the top. Belay on a good ledge 100 feet up or go to the anchors for *Giants of Science*. From the belay ledge, a short pitch will take you to the top, or you can traverse off to the south along an exposed third class ledge. Take a standard free rack.

Note: *Routes Q through W are located below the 4x4 Ledge. To reach the base, downclimb from the 4x4 Ledge to a narrow ledge system and traverse in from the north (third class). This downclimb is located below the boulder pile on the cliff prow north of the route. It is also possible to rappel **I Got Stripes** in order to reach the base.*

115

___**Q. Pass or Flail** 5.11d ★★★
If there is only one lesson you learn
from Schoolroom, make it this one.
This classic Greg Lowe route was first
free climbed in 1965. Only Macabre
Roof is more impressive when viewed
from a historical perspective. Use
powerful liebacking and strenuous,
awkward hand jams to ascend this 50-
foot, overhanging, thin, finger and hand
crack. Take a standard free rack with
a few small TCUs. This route can be
toproped but the belay must be built.

___**R. I Got Stripes** (project)
Sport route on the face right of *Pass
or Flail*. The route is 5.11 for the first
three bolts and then gets much harder.
The climbing is strenuous with tricky
and precise feet. When redpointed it
will probably be in the low 5.13 range.
Five bolts.

___**S. Monkey Wrench** 5.11a ★★
Fun, diverse climbing. Shares the anchor
with *UP & L*. Six bolts.

___**T. UP & L** 5.11d ★★★
Hard moves right off the ground lead
to easier climbing above the second
bolt. Shares an anchor with *Monkey
Wrench*. Six bolts.

___**U. Unnamed dihedral** 5.4
This route offers an alternative to the
22nd Street approach described above.
It can be started from the *Pass or Flail*
ledge or from the very base of the cliffband. A standard free rack is needed.

___**V. Propulsion** 5.12c ★★
New route. Six bolts

___**W. Project**

BNF AREA

This area is located at a recess in the Schoolroom Wall north of Central School-room where a shallow gully cuts the mountainside above the cliffband. It is constantly seeping water and sometimes forms good ice climbs in the winter. Most of the routes here are spread out along the right (south) side of the recess.

Approach: The recommended way is to follow the approach description for Central Schoolroom to *A Fist Full of Needles*. From there, hike north along the 4x4 Ledge for approximately 90 yards to a bit of a prow where the Pass or Flail area comes into view to the north. *Bad to the Bone* is on this prow to the right of a broken left-facing dihedral just before a big pile of boulders on the 4x4 Ledge. The other routes are just a little further north. This area can also be approached from Asbury Park, but it is a little more tricky and dangerous. For this approach follow the narrow lower ledges that form a meandering catwalk below the main 4x4 Ledge. They span from *BNF* to the Pass or Flail ledge and are often interrupted by obstacles. Expect some scary fourth class scrambling (see photo).

___**A. Spicy Tuna Roll** 5.12b ★★★

One of the best routes of its grade in the area. It is the left sport route on a prominent arête north of a big, left-facing dihedral. Beautiful face climbing leads to the exposed arête. Seven bolts.

___**B. For Whom the Bell Tolls 5.13a** ★★

Sport route to the right of *Spicy Tuna Roll*. Eight Bolts

___**C. No Talent Ass Clown** 5.10c ★★★

Fun climbing on excellent rock. One of the best 5.10s inthe area.

___**D. BNF** 5.11b ★★★

This route is located below the main 4x4 Ledge on an obvious arête. Although short, this four bolt route is of exceptional quality and well worth doing.

___**E. Bad to the Bone** 5.11 ★★

It's very rare to find a hand crack like this on the quartzite of Ogden. This slightly overhanging crack is nearly perfect for twenty feet. Smaller hands might make it easier. Watch out for dangerously loose rock just past the hand crack. Build a belay on a ledge 50 feet up. The original route descended a scary fifth class downclimb to the south, but the second pitch variation, *Universal Current*, is highly recommended. Take a standard free rack.

___**F. Universal Current** 5.8 ★★

Clean face and crack climbing starting from the righthand corner of the *Bad to the Bone* belay ledge. It follows the nice crack that splits the polished face above and to the right of *Bad to the Bone*. It can be done as a second pitch variation to *Bad to the Bone* or it can also be done from the ground in only one pitch by climbing up the former downclimb. Take a long runner to sling a big boulder on top to rappel off or you'll have to make a long hike south to the Tree Crack Area rappel bolts. A standard free rack is needed.

Bad to the Bone 5.11

Mike Anderson on BNF 5.11b   Photograph by Kelly Oldroyd

CENTRAL SCHOOLROOM

Central Schoolroom consists of only a few routes spread out over the large area located between the Tree Crack Area and the BNF Area. It hosts some of the only routes on the entire Schoolroom Wall on the lower half of the cliffband. Because the routes are so spread out, each area has an individual approach description.

___A. A Fist Full of Needles 5.7

Approach: Follow the Tree Crack Area approach description up to the 4x4 Ledge. From the 5.10 Slab, traverse north along the 4x4 Ledge for approximately 80 yards to where there is a small pile of boulders on the left. The route can't be missed. It is easily recognized as a fat crack in a left-facing dihedral. Most of the climbing is on the face using the crack for pro. At the top is an awkward spike of rock that makes things interesting. Take a standard free rack with extra cams in the 4 to 6 inch range. Build a belay on top and descend at one of the Tree Crack Area rappel stations.

Smith And Edwards

Smith And Edwards

801-731-1120

___**B. Corner Overhang** 5.10 / 5.11+ ★
Approach: Follow the approach description for *Strange Behavior*. From *Strange Behavior*, continue traversing north along the cliffband for approximately 30-40 yards until *Corner Overhang* comes into view. It is easily visible from the parking area.

Along with *Strange Behavior*, this is one of the few routes which climbs the lower half of the Schoolroom Wall and tops out on the 4x4 Ledge. There are three variations:

Variation 1: Bypass the overhang entirely by climbing straight up the face on the right before you even get under the roof (5.10). This is the easiest variation, but protection is scarce and the climbing isn't much fun.

Variation 2: Climb up the slab to the back corner of the overhang. Go straight up, stemming between the walls, until the horizontal crack beneath the roof is gained. Beware of a potential fall onto the slab (5.11).

Variation 3: Follow the slab up and left to the center of the overhang. Then, traverse right along the horizontal crack at the back of the roof, walking your gear as you go to prevent rope drag. This is the recommended option to get the most out of the route.

For variations two and three, exiting the overhang onto the main west face is the crux (5.11+). If possible, a double rope method of leading is recommended. Build a belay on top. Take a standard free rack with extra runners. Descend by hiking south to the Tree Crack Area.

___**C. Strange Behavior** 5.9 ★★
Approach: Follow the Tree Crack Area approach description up to the base of *Approach Crack* (pg 126, 133). From *Approach Crack*, traverse north along the cliff for approximately 90 yards as it angles slightly downhill. *Strange Behavior* is a vague route located at the back of a subtle alcove. As with *Corner Overhang*, this route climbs the lower half of the cliffband and tops out on the 4x4 Ledge.

Climb the dirty and tricky to protect corner up to a big detached block. Pass beneath the block to the crack on the right. Then, climb straight up to the diagonal finger and hand crack. Follow this crack to the 4x4 Ledge. The crux is exiting the diagonal crack. The belay must be built on top. Watch out for rope drag and don't forget to protect the follower. Be sure not to let your rope run over the **sharp edge** of the detached block. Take a standard free rack with a couple of extra fist sized cams. Nut placements are rare. Descend at the Tree Crack Area.

THE TANGERINE

Approach: Follow the approach description for the Tree Crack Area and then hike approximately fifty yards north of the 5.10 Slab (pg 127). The Tangerine is located just past the point where the 4x4 Ledge gets very narrow and then widens again. The rock quality here is impeccable.

___**A. Verona** 5.11a ★★★
Dynamic climbing up positive holds. Take a cam in the 1.75-inch range if you want to shorten the easy runout to the chains. Four bolts.

___**B. Excess Ain't Rebellion**
5.10b ★★★
The thin crack to the right of *Verona*. When the crack dies, angle left up the face to *Verona's* anchor. Take a standard free rack up to one inch.

___**C. Collateral Damage** 5.11c ★★
Climb past three bolts to a nice flake where clean gear will be needed. Then, follow two more bolts up a slab to a steep head wall. Five bolts and a standard free rack up to two inches.

___**D. BLU-82** 5.11a ★★★
Climb flakes and incut edges up to an easy slab and the steep headwall. Eight bolts.

The late Kent Jameson on Solar Flare 5.10

OVERVIEW OF TREE CRACK AREA

A. 510 Slab
B. Leaning Flake
C. Rocketsauce
D. Rappel Stateion

E. Tree Crack
F. Approach Crack
G. Psyche Corner

Approach: Park at the top (east end) of 27th Street. Take the trail heading east around the left side of the spillway. Work your way along assorted meandering trails to Castle Rock. Castle Rock can be identified as the very large boulder with white paint splattered down its west face. It resides halfway up the hillside at the base of the talus field, below the Schoolroom cliffband. On the north side of Castle Rock is a vague trail ascending into the talus field. Once in the talus field, the trail disappears. Head straight up aiming for the big flat boulders at the base of the cliffband. To gain the 4x4 Ledge, climb the *Approach Crack* (pg 133) located directly above the boulders or do a fourth class scramble located to the left of the Utahnics Wall (see Schoolroom Overview photo).

Descent: All routes that top out on the 4x4 Ledge can be descended at the single bolt *Approach Crack* anchor located below Tree Crack (60 feet). All routes that top out on the top of the upper cliffband, above the 4x4 Ledge, can be descended by using the Schoolroom South rappel station located directly above *Rocketsauce*. It is somewhat hidden beneath a small tree near the cliff edge. The rappel is 130 feet, so if you don't have two ropes, you'll have to rappel to the *Rocketsauce* anchor and then to the ground.

5.10 SLAB (NO PHOTO)

The 5.10 Slab is located on the face just to the left of Leaning Flake. It is on the far north end of the Tree Crack Area, just outside the left side of the Leaning Flake photo. (Leaning Flake is the massive detached flake at the north end of the Tree Crack Area. It makes a good landmark when looking for the area from the road).

___**A. Ladybug** 5.10b ★★

The crux at the third bolt has two options: Climb straight up for a challenge or move left to make it easier. Five bolts.

___**B. Mantis** 5.10c ★★

Climbers who surmount the blank-looking crux at the second bolt will be rewarded with fun moves in the crack above. Four bolts.

___**C. Body Count** 5.10a ★★

Though the climbing never gets very hard, you'll need your full concentration all the way up. Six bolts.

___**D. Attack on America** 5.10d ★★★

Dicey footwork leads to jugs above. Six bolts.

TREE CRACK AREA

The Tree Crack Area is the all-you-can-eat-buffet of the Schoolroom Wall. While many of the routes here are desperate, there are also several moderates (5.10 or less) to choose from. This area should not be missed by any self-respecting Ogden climber. Besides the routes listed, there is also a fun fifth class chimney behind the flake and a short second pitch from the top of the flake onto the main wall.

___**A. Tigers and Vaseline** 5.12c ★★★
Three bolt sport route on the north arête of the Leaning Flake.

___**B. Mercury Topaz** 5.12a ★★
Sport route on the far left side of the west face of Leaning Flake. Expect steep, sustained climbing on in-cut holds for six bolts.

___**C. Mr. Styles** 5.10b ★★
Start on the right-arching flake and follow a continuous stream of jugs up the steep face. Fun and healthy climbing for five bolts.

Mark Anderson on Mr. Styles 5.10b   Photograph by Mike Anderson

___**D. Lickety Split** 5.11c ★
A difficult start leads to easier climbing after the second bolt. Positive edges and sidepulls abound if you can find them. Seven bolts.

___**E. Rehab's for Quitters** 5.9 ★★
Big holds and quality rock. Five bolts.

___**F. South Ridge Direct** 5.10+ ★★★
A harder variation to the start of the *South Ridge*. Clip a bolt at the base and then use big holds to pull the roof onto the *South Ridge*.

___**G. South Ridge** 5.6 ★★
The right arête of the Leaning Flake. Take a standard free rack.

TREE CRACK AREA NORTH

___**H. Ethics** 5.8 ★★
Quality face climbing on big holds. Climb past three bolts then continue straight up to a bolt anchor using horizontal cracks for pro. The final stretch is a little runout to the anchor. The first ascensionists originally planned to bolt the entire route. After drilling the third bolt, they realized there were plenty of horizontal cracks for pro. Following a short debate, they ceased drilling. Hence, the route name. Take a standard free rack and few extra TCUs.

___**I. Jammin' For Jesus** 5.10b ★★
This is the thin seam between *Phat Abbot* and *Ethics*. It consists of fun face climbing with the crack used mostly just for gear. Take a standard free rack up to two inches as well as thin gear and micro-nuts.

___**J. Phat Abbot** 5.11c ★★
Climb the polished slab using sloping crimps. Six bolts.

___**K. Solar Flare Direct Start** 5.10d R ★
This bold variation to *Solar Flare* has a difficult start protected only by old and unreliable pitons. There is a good stance 20 feet up where the climbing gets easier, but protection is sparse and questionable. The slot/corner near the top offers the first good protection of the entire route — 60 feet up.

___**L. Solar Flare** 5.10 ★★
Climb a strenuous finger and hand crack up a steep face and then angle left up the slab to the slot/corner. This well-protected and challenging corner has intriguing chimney and stemming moves you won't find anywhere else. Build a belay on top. Take a standard free rack. Descend by using the Tree Crack Area rappel.

___**M. Cremegenes** 5.10d ★
This is an alternate finish to *Solar Flare*. Instead of angling left into the slot, continue straight up some fun flakes to a bolt anchor. Another good variation angles left across more flakes just before the *Creamgenes* anchor to the slot finish of *Solar Flare*.

___**N. Rocketsauce** 5.11c ★★★
Exciting moves lead over the left side of the overhanging face in the center of the Tree Crack Area. The climbing eases off on the slab, but save some strength for the upper head wall. Ten bolts.

___**O. Shiny Demon** 5.9+ ★★★
This is an alternate finish to either
Rocketsauce or *Solar Flare*. It follows a wild,
right-angling crack from the ledge at
the eighth bolt of *Rocketsauce*. It can be
done in one pitch, but an intermediate
belay on the slab will reduce rope drag.
Take a standard free rack and two or
three TCUs.

___**P. Castrated Stalker** 5.12d ★★★
This route powers over the middle of
the overhanging face in the center of
the wall. Excellent rock and big moves.
Six bolts.

___**Q. Wish it Were Granite** 5.9 ★★
This route adds a fun second pitch
to *Castrated Stalker*. It follows the left-
angling crack directly over the anchor to
finish on *Shiny Demon*. Take a standard
free rack.

___**R. Explosivo** 5.11d ★★★
Starts on the right side of the overhanging face in the middle of the wall
with forceful moves to a flake. Technical
climbing on the slab above leads to an
overhanging finish on jugs. Ten bolts.

___**S. Rockprodigy** 5.12a ★★★
Steep and powerful climbing. There is
a second pitch that has yet to be sent.
Five bolts. Photo following page.

TREE CRACK AREA SOUTH

___T. Macondo 5.9 ★★

Begin by scrambling up to a small ledge at the base of the route. Climb a fun well-protected flake up to a series of ledges. The gear gets a little sparse through the ledges but the climbing is easy. Then, stem and lie-back up the excellent corner system. Belay at the bolts on the top of the corner. A 100-foot rappel will get you to the ground or a short second pitch will take you to the top. Take a standard free rack.

___U. The Wasp 5.12c ★★

Thin and consistent sport climbing on the face left of *Tree Crack*. It relents to 5.11 for the last 20 feet. Seven bolts.

___V. Tastes Like Burning 5.10d ★★★

Good face climbing up to the *Tree Crack* anchors. Six bolts.

___W. Tree Crack 5.11a ★★★

The crux is the finger crack right off the deck. Involved sequences and awkward moves get progressively easier as you near the top. The protection is good and the climbing fun. Belay at the tree or continue to the top for some more good climbing. Take a standard free rack with a couple of TCUs to protect the start. Descend by rappelling from the tree or using the Schoolroom south rappel if you topped out.

___X. Breakfast of Champions
5.12d ★★★

This route shares the start of *Tree Crack* before moving right onto the face for the first bolt. The face consists of relentless powerful climbing with no rests until the last bolt. A direct start to the right might be possible, but do not add any bolts because *Tree Crack* will certainly be compromised. Take a few TCUs to protect the start. Five bolts.

___Y. Goodbye Blue Monday
5.12a ★★★

Start on the ledge at the base of *Tree Crack* and climb the dihedral up to the first bolt. You'll need a couple of TCUs if you don't want to run it out. The rest of the route climbs the smooth face to the left of *Breakfast of Champions*. Six bolts and a few TCUs. by using the Tree Crack Area rappel.

___Z. Psyche Corner 5.10 **R** ★

For this vague route, start up the easy ledges right of *Tree Crack* and aim for the black-colored flakes halfway up the face. After the flakes, a good ledge is gained where you can sit back and contemplate the beautiful, splitter hand crack spanning the next 15 feet to the top. Watch out for some very big and very dangerous loose rock at the summit. The belay on top must be built. Take a standard free rack. Descend by using the Tree Crack Area rappel.

___AA. Approach Crack 5.7

(See Tree Crack Area Overview photo, pg 126) This crack provides a fun way to reach the 4x4 Ledge instead of doing the scramble. Take a standard free rack and belay on top at a single bolt anchor.

UTAHNICS WALL

The Utahnics Wall is located just to the right of the approach scramble for the Tree Crack Area. There are a few moderate sport routes here which are rare in Ogden. All routes can be toproped by doing the Tree Crack Area approach scramble to the left of *Hype Dependent*. These routes also provide a fun way to gain access to the 4x4 Ledge if approaching the Tree Crack Area.

Approach: Follow the approach description for the Tree Crack Area and then traverse south a short distance along the base of the cliffband. It is located at a point where the main cliffband begins to wrap east into Taylor's Canyon (see the Schoolroom Wall Overview Photo, pg 109).

___A. Hype Dependent 5.12a ★★
Scramble up easy ledges to ledge below
the arête. A big dyno is followed by big
holds to the top. Don't blow it on the
second clip. Four bolts.

___B. Diamondback 5.9 ★
This route is named after the snake the
first ascensionists unknowingly flaked
their rope on. Climb the crack in the
back of the obvious dihedral. Take a
standard free rack.

___C. Utahnics 5.10a ★
Big holds on the mottled face.
Five bolts.

___D. Holy Moroni 5.8 ★
More big holds. Five bolts.

___E. Oh My Nephi 5.8 ★
Shares the start of *Holy Moroni* and then
angles right after the first bolt. Five
bolts.

___F. The Good Ward 5.6 ★
Meandering trad route right of the
others. Take a standard free rack.

TAYLOR'S CORNER AREA

This is the only area on the wall that can not be reached by the 4x4 Ledge. It is easily recognized by the giant, right arcing corner at the south end of the wall not far from Taylor's Canyon.

Approach: Follow the approach description for The Tree Crack Area. Upon reaching the base of the cliff, traverse south along the top of the scree slope until directly below *27th Street Overhang* — easily recognized as the big, arch-shaped roof. Do an easy scramble up to the base of the overhang and traverse south along a ledge to reach *Taylor's Corner*.

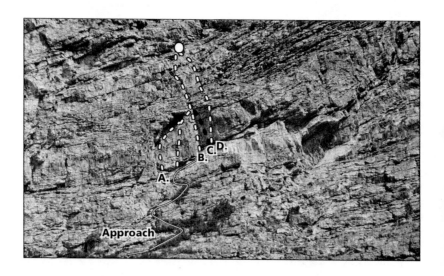

___A. 27th Street Overhang

Although this route has reportedly been climbed, not much information is currently available. It begins in the corner and follows the arch out to the right until it connects with *Taylor's Corner*. Finish on *Taylor's Corner*. It looks like an exciting and unique route worth the effort of a competent leader. The face beneath the roof has also been reported as being climbed in 1964.

___B. Taylor's Corner 5.8 ★★

To the right of the *27th Street Overhang* is a triangular apron of rock which forms a right-facing dihedral on its south side. *Taylor's Corner* climbs the face of this apron. It does not begin in the dihedral to the right and is a little difficult to protect until the corner is gained. There are, however, a few fixed pins to help ease your mind. Fun face climbing leads to interesting stemming in the dihedral above. Belay on top where a big boulder can be slung. Two ropes are needed to rappel the route. Take a standard free rack and a few TCUs to help protect the start.

___C. Boxelder Salsa 5.10c ★★

The left-facing dihedral to the right of the start of *Taylor's Corner* and left of *Laurel*. Named after the hundreds of boxelder bugs who gave their lives during the first ascent of this route. Follow the crack to a few bolts on the face and then finish on *Taylor's Corner*. Take a standard free rack.

___D. Laurel 5.8 C2

This is an extremely thin crack on the white face a few feet right of *Taylor's Corner*. Take a standard free rack with several micro nuts, TCUs, and any clean aid tricks you know. The final 20 feet are 5.8. The route shares the anchor for *Taylor's Corner*.

___E. Ana 5.8 ★

This route is located south of *Taylor's Corner* where the Schoolroom Wall wraps east around the corner to form the mouth of Taylor's Canyon. It faces south. At five pitches, it is by far the longest route on the Schoolroom Wall. Pitch five is the hardest and a bit tricky to protect. All anchors must be built. Walk off to the Tree Crack Area rappel. Take a standard free rack.

THE SEVEN

The Seven is the limestone crag located on the south side of the mouth of Taylor's Canyon. This is one of the areas where the Lowes first learned to climb as kids in the 1950s. It is currently home to only two routes, but more are likely to go up due to the excellent quality of the limestone. It faces northwest and so receives morning shade and afternoon sun. The approach is steep, but worth the trouble.

Approach: Park at the top of 27th Street where the road dead ends at the mountainside. The Seven is the prominent crag on the south side of the mouth of Taylor's Canyon and is easily seen from the parking area. There is a maze of trails in this area, but you should be able to find your way without trouble. Hike primarily east along assorted meandering trails until you are directly below the crag. At this point the trail disappears and you must hike straight up the loose slope. *Voluntary Poverty* ascends the center of the lower face while *Quiet Desperation* is located on a big ledge above.

___A. Voluntary Poverty 5.9 TR ★
This route is the toprope which climbs the center of the lower wall. It consists of good face and slab climbing. It makes a good warm up for an attempt on *Quiet Desperation*. It has a bolted anchor located on the ledge below *Quiet Desperation*.

___B. Unnamed (project)
There are anchors for an abandoned project located on the left end of the overhang.

___C. Quiet Desperation (project)
This route was first aided by the Lowes (as kids with their father) when they were first learning to climb in the 1950s. It has since seen several failed free attempts . The route begins on the upper ledge above *Voluntary Poverty* and pulls the huge roof via the obvious splitter hand crack. It then continues straight up the face using a few diagonal and horizontal cracks for protection. It seeps in the early spring making it unclimbable for a short time. There is a bolted anchor on top.

Approach

29TH STREET

This southwest facing area gets morning shade. These short but fun routes are great when you need to get a quick fix and can't stomach another day at 9th Street.

Approach: Park at the trailhead at the top (east end) of 29th Street. The crag is visible from the parking lot. It is located directly east of the trailhead in a small gully. Take the trail that climbs southeast up the hillside. When you hit the power line road, head north until you pass a power pole on the right. From this point, follow a vague trail straight up into the gully to the base of the crag. Approach time is only 10 minutes.

___**A. Safety Goggles** 5.9 ★
A short two-bolt route up a mottled face. Good toprope.

___**B. Overlooked** 5.10a ★★
This is the best route on the wall. Three bolts up a nice face.

___**C. 8 Ball in the Corner** 5.8
Climb the obvious corner and pass the roof on the left. High first bolt. Shares an anchor with *Loose Shingles*. Three bolts.

___**D. Loose Shingles** 5.10d ★
This route tackles the roof head on. Four bolts.

Greg Reynolds on Safety Goggles 5.9   Photograph by David G. Robb

ECHO CANYON

Many climbers have driven through Echo Canyon and stared up at the beautiful red cliffs to the north, wondering what possibilities they held. A hike to their base, however, reveals that the rock quality is about as poor as it gets before its called dirt. These routes offer a few exceptions.

Approach: Take I-84 east up Weber Canyon for approximately 30 miles. When the freeway splits take I-80 east toward Cheyenne and then quickly take the first exit (#169). Turn left at the bottom of the exit and drive beneath the freeway to a "T" in the road. For The Sentinel turn left to Echo and for all other routes turn right on Echo Canyon Road. See the individual route approaches for further information.

The Sentinel
pg 141

	5.0-5.7	5.8	5.9	5.10	5.11	5.12	5.13	5.14
I								

Monument Rock
pg 142

	5.0-5.7	5.8	5.9	5.10	5.11	5.12	5.13	5.14
I								

Echo Canyon Arête
pg 142

Project not rated

5.0-5.7	5.8	5.9	5.10	5.11	5.12	5.13	5.14

Three Day Plan (A0)
pg 143

	5.0-5.7	5.8	5.9	5.10	5.11	5.12	5.13	5.14
			I		I			

THE SENTINEL

The Sentinel is a chimney-like spire located 1.5 miles west from the "T" in the road mentioned above. Drive through the town of Echo and watch for a historical marker on the right. Park at the historical marker and hike north for 20-30 minutes to the Sentinel. It is easily visible from the road.

___**A. South Face** 5.8 R
Face climb the obvious weaknesses up the south side of the spire. There is one bolt which should be visible from the ground. Take a standard free rack and a few pitons (mainly angles) to help protect where the clean gear can't.

MONUMENT ROCK

___B. Monument Rock
(North Ridge) 5.7

Monument Rock is the obvious free standing spire located in a gully 0.1 of a mile east on Echo Canyon Road from the above mentioned "T" (see Echo Canyon approach, pg 141). It is climbed from a notch on the back (north) side. Approach by hiking around the right side in order to avoid some scrambling. The exciting summit contains some antique-looking anchors. The first ascent must have been many years ago.

___C. Unknown 5.12c
This bolt ladder climbs the striking south face. Rock quality is marginal, but the position isamazing.

ECHO CANYON ARÊTE

___D. Echo Canyon Arête (projects)
The Arête is probably the most stunning feature in the area. It is located 1.4 miles east on Echo Canyon Road from the above mentioned "T" (see Echo Canyon approach, pg 141). There are two unfinished sport routes on the gently overhanging prow which look to be of good quality and high difficulty.

THREE DAY PLAN DIHEDRAL

___E. Three Day Plan
5.11 or 5.9 A0 ★

Approach: *Three Day Plan* is located on an enormous dihedral which can't be missed. To reach it, drive 2.3 miles east on Echo Canyon Road from the above mentioned "T" and the dihedral will come into view on the left. Park at a fenced utility shed on the right and hike straight up. This route is not for the faint hearted. The rock is made up of occasional layers of extremely soft sandstone (this is the good stuff) between layers of dangerously loose conglomerate rock. Although there is a nice crack to place protection in, it is often questionable. Most of the route is 5.9 with only two or three moves of 5.11 which is fairly easy to "French free." Absolutely, positively do not go anywhere near this thing if it has rained within a week.

1st Pitch: Climb the left of two cracks through a corner up to a loose, dirty ledge to gain the main dihedral. Jam and lieback your way up the dihedral to a belay in a layer of the better rock about 50 feet above the ledge. This belay must be built.

2nd Pitch: Continue up the crack to a prominent roof. Pull the roof on the lower right side (5.11) and move up onto the face where there is a fixed pin.

It is a little runout until the crack can be regained. Follow the crack to a three bolt belay.

3rd Pitch: Jam, lieback, and face climb your way to one of the coolest belays and enjoy the view.

4th Pitch: The fourth and final pitch is not recommended. It traverses to the right from the belay, is 5.7, and is somewhat runout. Descend by walking off to the east. If descending from the top of the third pitch, two double rope repels will return you to safety. Take a double set of cams up to a #4 Camalot, and a set of nuts.

DRY WALL

The Dry Wall is located 2.8 miles east on Echo Canyon Road from the above mentioned "T." It is recognized as a slightly overhanging graffitied face to the west of a gully. There are Maple Canyon-type sport routes of good quality that stay dry even when it's raining. A stick-clip is recommended.

___**A. J. J. Memorial** 5.12c ★★★
Seven bolts.

___**B. The Pit** 5.12c ★★
Stick-clip recommended.

___**C. Wicked Bender** 5.13a ★★
Excellent variation of B that angles left
at the third bolt to end on *J.J. Memorial.*

___**D. Graffiti Patient** 5.12b ★★
Five bolts. A nice variation ends on E.

___**E. Way Hammered** 5.12c
Seven bolts.

___**F. Grushenka** 5.12c

___**G. Stop That Terrain** 5.12c ★★

___**H. Pocket Full of Trundles** 5.11b/c
★★★
Pocket and cobble climbing. Seven bolts
and a chain anchor.

___**I. Something Must Break** 5.12a
More pockets and cobbles. Seven bolts and
a chain anchor.

___**J. The Whole Shibang** 5.13ac ★★
This route begins on I and traverses the
entire face to end on A.

___**K. The Lowe Route** 5.10c ★
Six bolts.

___**L. Can't Say** 5.10a
Six bolts.

___**M. The Precious** 5.10b ★

___**N. Little Red Rooster** 5.12c ★
Four bolts.

CAUSEY RESERVOIR

Excellent limestone (the best anywhere in this book by far), hard sport routes, and a serene setting make Causey a sport climbers dream come true. This place has everything from slabs to massive overhangs. Some of the approaches, though a little long, are quite pleasant. This is a nice place to hike even if your not climbing. Many of the walls seep in the spring so the best seasons are early summer and fall. Active development means you can expect more routes in the future on both the areas listed below and ones not mentioned here. All routes are bolted. Each area has an individual approach description.

Approach: From the Pineview Dam at the top of Ogden Canyon, continue 5.6 miles to the Monte Cristo turn-off. Turn right and follow the Monte Cristo road up South Fork Canyon for nine miles. Turn right at the Causey Dam road and follow it to where it dead ends at Camp Kiesel. Do not cross the Causey Dam. Park just outside of the gate for Camp Kiesel. The climbing areas are located up Wheat Grass Canyon from Camp Kiesel. Approximate drive time from Ogden is 40 minutes.

Hair Dog Wall pg 147

5.0-5.7	5.8	5.9	5.10	5.11	5.12	5.13	5.14
				I	4	2	

The Kamakazi Wall pg 148

5.0-5.7	5.8	5.9	5.10	5.11	5.12	5.13	5.14
I				I	2		

Serendipity Wall pg 150

5.0-5.7	5.8	5.9	5.10	5.11	5.12	5.13	5.14
		2			7	2	

Vampire Cave pg 152

5.0-5.7	5.8	5.9	5.10	5.11	5.12	5.13	5.14
				I	I	4	3

Dragons Lair pg 154

6 or 7 projects in the 5.13/5.14 range

5.0-5.7	5.8	5.9	5.10	5.11	5.12	5.13	5.14

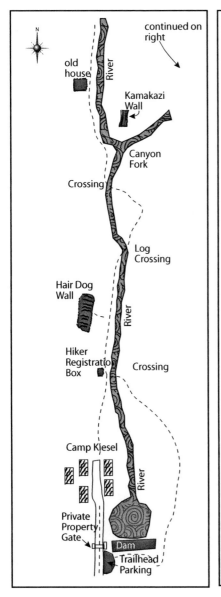

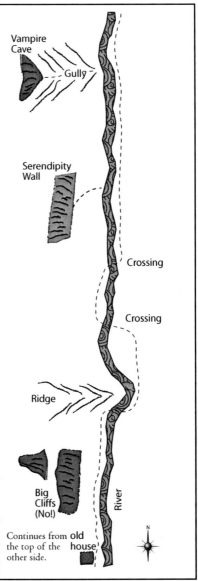

147

HAIR DOG WALL

This is the first and easiest area to reach in Wheat Grass Canyon. It is very close to the trail and is noted for the three big overhangs that dominate the wall. The rock here is not nearly as good as further up, but some of the routes are of decent quality.

Approach: From the parking lot outside the gate of Camp Kiesel, cross the small dam and take the lefthand fork of the trail. Follow this trail as it traverses the hillside above Camp Kiesel. It soon drops back into the canyon and crosses the river. Approximately 100 yards after you cross the river Hair Dog Wall will appear on the left side of the canyon. The wall is about 30 yards off the trail. Approach time is around 15-20 minutes.

___**A. A Time To Bleed** 5.13b

___**B. Joey's Route of Science** 5.13b

Note: *Routes C and D end at a bail 'biner beneath the final roof. The roof was never sent.*

___**C. Rat Face and Putty Boy** 5.12c

___**D. Hair Dogs** 5.12a ★

___**E. Turning Into Putty** 5.12c

___**F. Mono** 5.12b/c

___**G. La Arena** 5.10c ★★

THE KAMAKAZI WALL (no photo)

The Kamakazi Wall is a tiny crag perched on the shoulder overlooking the fork where Bear Hollow and Wheatgrass Canyon come together. It hosts four routes of pretty good quality. Like Hair Dog Wall, it is not as good as the areas higher up the canyon, but it is worth stopping by. Routes are listed from left to right.

Approach: Follow the approach description for Hair Dog Wall, but continue hiking up canyon. After hiking around 10 minutes the canyon will fork. Bear Hollow is the right fork and Wheat Grass Canyon is the left. Take the lefthand fork. The Kamakazi Wall is located high on the shoulder between the two canyons and is recognized as a small tower of white limestone with black streaks. It is a bit of a bush-whack to the base about 150-200 yards up the hillside. Approach time is around 25-30 minutes.

Note: *Routes A and B are on the west face and C and D are on the south.*

___**A. Rage Against the Scene** 5.12d ★   ___**C. Kate's Ho Ho** 5.11a

___**B. Mr. Kamakazi** 5.12c ★   ___**D. In the Deap** 5.7 ★★

SERENDIPITY WALL

The Serendipity Wall is the centerpiece of the Causey Area. It has a high concentration of routes on excellent limestone, mostly in the 5.12 to 5.13 range. This crag offers some of the best sport climbing anywhere in this guide, featuring massive overhangs, steep faces and slabs. Don't bother travelling to Logan or American Fork, this is where you need to be.

Approach: Follow the approach description to the Kamakazi Wall, but continue up the lefthand canyon for approximately 20 minutes. The wall is on the left side of the canyon about 200 yards up the hillside. It is visible through the trees from the canyon trail. Keep walking until you are just starting to pass the crag before you cut up the hillside. There is usually a cairn built at the start of a vague trail leading up to the wall. Approach time is 45-50 minutes.

___**A. Project** (no photo)

___**B. Project** (no photo)

___**C. Project**

___**D. Project**

___**E. Black Streak** (project)

___**F. Social Values** 5.13a ★★★

___**G. Turbulent Mirror** 5.13b ★★★

___**H. Petrified** 5.12c ★★

___**I. Hierarchy** 5.12b ★★★

___**J. Don't Tread on Me** 5.12a ★★★

___**K. In Harms Way** 5.12a

___**L. The Scandal** 5.12b ★

___**M. Kill the Rat** 5.12d ★★

___**N. Project**

___**O. Grey Matter** 5.12b ★

___**P. Black Pudding** 5.9 ★

___**Q. Lung Chowder** 5.9 ★

VAMPIRE CAVE

Is the Serendipity Wall not steep or hard enough? Then you might want to give the Vampire Cave a try. Just a short jaunt up canyon from Serendipity is this severely overhanging cave. With the exception of one 5.11, everything in here is HARD. Bouldery and powerful climbing on crimpy holds pull over thirty feet of overhanging rock. It should be noted that there are two routes in the cave that are chipped: *Bloodless Corpse* has two chipped holds and *Black Knowledge* has one chipped hold. These are the only routes in the area with chipped holds and this should not be considered the standard or even acceptable.

Approach: Follow the approach description to the Serendipitty Wall, but continue hiking up the canyon. Not far after the cut-off to the Serendipitty Wall the trail cuts back to the left side of the river. Twenty yards past the river crossing the trail leading up to the Vampire Cave will cut off to the left. There is usually a cairn marking the cut-off for the vague trail. The Vampire Cave is not easily seen from the canyon trail, but it is the very next crag on the hillside past the Serendipitty Wall. Be sure not to pass it and mistakenly go to the big cliffs up canyon. Approach time is around one hour.

Anthony Chertudi on Out Come the Wolves

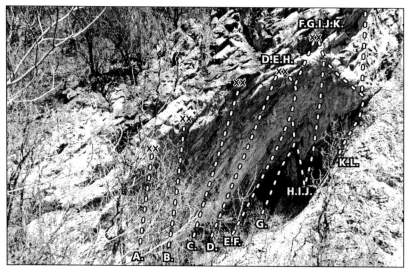

___**A. Vicious Cycle** 5.11a

___**B. Head Chopper** 5.12d

___**C. Maldito Duende** 5.13b/c ★★★

___**D. Bloodless Corpse (project)**

___**E. White Terror** 5.14a ★★

___**F. Black Knowledge** 5.14b ★★★

___**G. Vampire Direct (project)**

___**H. Feeding Off Life** 5.13d ★★

___**I. Vampire Cafe** 5.14a ★★★

___**J. Out Come the Wolves (project)**

___**K. Nos Vertue** 5.13c/d

___**L. Madness is Now** 5.13b ★★

Jed Lowe on Bloodless Corpse
Photo by Anthony Chertudi

DRAGONS LAIR (no photo)

Expect excellent limestone and a 45 degree, 40 foot long overhang with six or seven sport routes. All routes are currently open projects in the 5.13 to 5.14 range. The cliffband the Dragons Lair is located on is a mile long and has lots of potential for future routes. The solitude and scenery alone make it worth the hike.

Approach: The Dragons Lair is also in Wheatgrass Canyon, but it is not reached by hiking up from Causey Reservoir like the other areas. Instead, it is much easier to reach by hiking down Wheatgrass Canyon from above. To get there, drive an additional 13 miles past the turn-off for Causey Reservoir, up to the top of Monte Cristo along Hwy 39. The gravel turn-off is a little hard to see, so be sure to watch your mileage. It is located on the right side of the road on a sharp turn with a passing lane. Once you turn off, a sign reads *Motor Vehicles On Roads Only*. Drive down the dirt road until it dead ends at a loop and park there. The road is a bit rough and will require a high clearance vehicle. Hike down the trail leading downhill to the south along the top of Elk Ridge for approximately 25-30 minutes. The trail gets more and more vauge as you go, but there's only one, so you shouldn't loose it. When you come to a big *No Trespassing* sign nailed to a tree on the right, with a smaller yellow sign that reads *Cooperative Wildlife Management Unit Boundery* under it, then you've gone twenty yards too far. At this point, cut down the hill to the left (east) that drops into Wheatgrass Canyon. There is no real trail here, but you should be in a shallow hollow filled with aspens. It soon steepens and opens up to where there is a deep rocky slot in the cliffband. Drop down through this slot and the Dragons Lair will appear on the right as you come out. You have to scramble up to a nice ledge beneath the cave to reach the routes. Approach time is around 45 minutes.

ST. JOE'S BOULDER FIELD by Brent Hadley

This is one of Ogden's most prized jems, located on the city's east bench and stretching from 22nd Street on the north to 27th Street on the south, directly below the Schoolroom Wall. In the 1970s the boulderfield was originally called St. Joe's, but in recent years it has become known as the 26th Street Boulderfield. However, since all access to the boulders has been blocked on 26th Street, I have reverted back to the original name.

Dozens of boulders and over 100 routes arre documented. Many more routes have been done, but all could not be listed. The routes included in the guide were chosen for their purity of line, but endless variations exist.

All the boulders are quartzite and are noted for their crimpy edges, polished surfaces, and occasional cracks. Most of the landings are good and the typical boulder height is about 10 feet. The ratings are subjective and should be taken with a grain of salt. The average rating is V4 or less, but problems up to V9 exist. Most of the boulders have casual approaches and the thick scrub oak offers ample shade. This is a great winter bouldering area due to the west-facing hillside and relatively low altitude. Mid-summer gets a little hot, except in the mornings.

The maps provided should only be considered a rough guide, as the complicated network of trails spread throughout the boulderfield is nearly impossible to to chart. Plan on getting lost a few times if you have never been to the boulderfield or when searching for new boulders.

Please observe the traditional ethics of this area and do not chip, glue, or otherwise deface the rock in any way and clean up all tick marks and chalk. In order to keep the area enjoyable for everyone, please pack out trash (even if it's not yours), stay on the main trails to prevent erosion, and be respectful of the local residents and hikers to prevent access issues. Lastly, a few of the boulders contain pictographs — in order to prevent possible damage, avoid climbing near the ancient art.

Other bouldering areas include the Weber High Boulder Area, below the Nature Center Wall, the 9th Street Area, and the mouth of South Fork Canyon on the way to the Causey area (Hwy 39).

Be aware that poison ivy, prickly pears, rattlesnakes, and wasps are found in abundance in the foothills of Ogden.

Approach: All boulders can be accessed from the top (east end) of either 24th Street or 27th Street. The 27th Street trailhead seems to be the most useful. 26th Street can no longer be used due to a home being built on the trailhead. From these trailheads, use the maps to find the boulders you want.

LOWER BOULDER FIELD

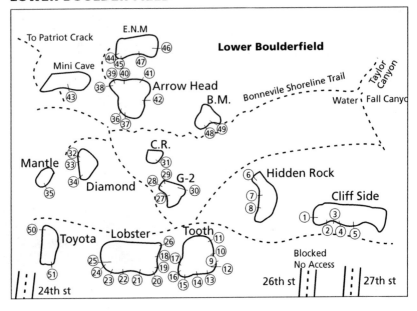

CLIFFSIDE

___**1. Gygi Traverse** V5 ★★

North to south follows seam finish in scoop.

___**2. Young Lust** V1

Climbs corner.

___**3. Hey You** V2

Climbs right along rail.

___**4. Vera** V1

___**5. Numb** V3

Starts on small crimps; hard feet.

HIDDEN ROCK (popular boulder for eliminates)

___**6. Hidden Rock Traverse** V2 ★★

Traverse east staying under the roof; turn corner.

___**7. Transmission** V1 ★

Follows the crack.

___**8. Disorder** V2 ★★

 Climbs up small crimps over the roof.

THE TOOTH

___**9. Passover** V1
Climbs arête.

___**10. Dead Sun** V2 ★★★
Straight up the face avoiding arête with
hands and feet.

___**11. Shore Leave** V1
 Climbs arête.

___**12. Tooth Traverse** V4 ★★
Starts by #9. Traverse south to north
finish on #16.

___**13. Liar** V6
L under cling, R sharp tooth, slap ramp
and mantle.

 ___**14. Singapore** V3
Follow the seam.

___**15. Mecham** V4 ★★
L crimp, R sloper, big move R
hand finish up arête.

___**16. November** V1
Start on ramp; climb up to loose block

___**17. Lichen** V2
Start on ramp; climbs out left on
lichen face.

LOBSTER

___**18. Six Foot and Curly** V4 ★★
Starts on slopers; R hand big move
to crimp.

___**19. Sixteen Shells** V1
Follows the seams to the right of
the corner.

___**20. Lobster Ar^te** V2 ★★★
Climbs arête; fun finish.

___**21. Pony** V4
Climbs small crimps.

___**22. Blue** V1
Climbs up the corner.

___**23. Breed** V1
Climbs small crack.

___**24. Dyno** V2
Dyno around the corner from #23.

___**25. Lobster Traverse** V3
Traverse north to south; finish on #19.

___**26. Johnny** V3
Double-handed dyno.

G-2

___**27. G-2** V0
Start by G-2 painted on the rock.

___**28. P.P.** V2
Start on big sloper.

___**29. 220** V2 ★
Same start as #28; L goes to edge
out left.

___**30. P.P. Traverse** V2 ★★
Traverse lip south to north.

157

C.R.

___31. Randall V4 ★

L crimp, R pinch, work your way up arête; sharp.

DIAMOND

___32. Negative V2 ★★

Start on underclings; climb arête.

___33. Black Market V3

Same start as #33; R goes to sloper finish out on arête.

___34. Creep V1 ★

Climb arête.

MANTLE

___35. Bottom Feeder V1

Trees are thick at the base.

ARROWHEAD

___36. Slick 50 V8 ★★★

Starts on underclings; turns slab out left.

___37. Slick 50 Direct V9 ★★★

Same start as #36. Climbs arête instead of turning onto slab.

___38. Checker V2 ★

Bad landing. Start on arêtes; go to jug out left.

___39. STP V2 ★

Bad landing. Start on jug; climbs out right toward arête.

___40. Lock Tight V3 ★★

Start on edge at eye level; climbs straight up face.

___41. WD-40 V4 ★★

Crimpy moves; finish out left on arête.

___42. 5.7 Slab ★★★

Pretty black face. This is the down-climb.

MINI CAVE

___43. Mini Cave V4 ★★

Starts on big hold; matched L; big move to lip.
Project: traverse lip.

E.N.M.

___44. Taddy V5 ★★

Climbs arête out left.

___45. Paulaner V5★

Climbs arête out right.

___46. E.S.B. V6 ★

Traverse south to north; finish on #45.

___47. Stout V4★★

Dyno.

B.M.

___**48. Poison** V2
Climb out right.

___**49. Ivy** V1
Climb out left.

TOYOTA

___**50. Crystal** V3 ★
Short route; start on small crimps; big move to lip.

___**51. Toyota Traverse** V1
Traverse lip.

Jodi Dawson on Tooth Boulder   Photograph by Ruth Robb

PATRIOT CRACK AREA

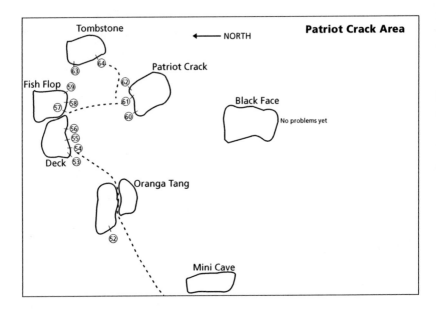

ORANGUTAN

___**52. Bob** V3 ★

 Climb arête; easier finish if you top out left.

THE DECK

___**53. Skoal** V1

Start chest high; climbs over orange rock scar.

___**54. Drum** V2

Same start as #53; climbs right on slopers.

___**55. Crimper** V3 ★★

R undercling, L crimp, head out left to small crimp in the crack.

___**56. Cancer** V0

Fish flop.

___**57. Buddha** V5 ★★★

 R small crimp, L sidepull crimp; big move; finish up on slopers.

___**58. Fish Flop** V2 ★★★

Start on big hold; climb left then straight up face.

___**59. Golden** V2

Same start as #58; climbs out right by arête.

(easier routes on east face)

PATRIOT CRACK

___**60. Suicide Crack** V3 ★★★

 Climbs crack.

___**61. Patriot Crack** V2 ★★

 Pulls little roof; follows crack.

___**62. Spine** V2

  Start on ramp; climbs left side of arête.

TOMBSTONE

___**63. LCC** V3 ★★

Climb arête.

___**64. Pain Train** V3 ★

Painful finger lock; climbs to big hold middle of face.

UPPER BOULDER FIELD

THE GORN

___**65. The Gorn** V6 ★★★

Start in undercling crack; route trends left.

C.V.

___**66. The Boot** V4 ★★

  Starts on crimps; pulls roof out right.

A-5

This boulder is south of C.V. down in the talus.

___**67. Shout at the Devil** V3 ★

Starts on underclings; big move to lip.

26TH

___**68. Second Rate** V3

 Climbs out roof; east-facing.

CASTLE ROCK

___**69. West Face** 5.10d

Toprope problem on west face.

AROUND THE WORLD

A great boulder for eliminates; south-west-facing

___**70. Traverse** V3

Traverse west to east.

___**71. Power** V3

Climbs just left of arête on west face; big moves.

___**72. Flapper** V1

Starts on a big jug; climbs left to sharp crimp.

___**73. Sunny Days** V1

Same start as #72; traverse up high and right.

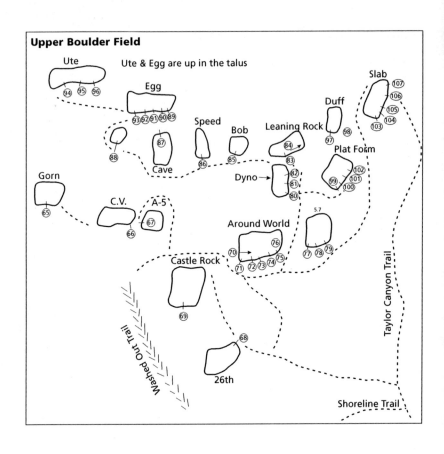

Upper Boulder Field

Ute & Egg are up in the talus

Ute
Egg
Speed
Bob
Leaning Rock
Duff
Slab
Plat Form
Gorn
Cave
Dyno →
C.V.
A-5
Around World
5.7
Castle Rock
26th
Washed Out Trail
Taylor Canyon Trail
Shoreline Trail

___**74. BW** V3

Starts on big holds; L goes to mail box slot, R to tooth, punch out left to crimps top-out.

___**75. Thumb** V4

 Climbs to sloping ramp; L goes to Gaston in black rock; hit lip.

___**76. Chopper** V0

Climb big holds traversing right.

___5.7 **Note:** *Tall boulder; fun routes*

___**77. Jury** V1

___**78. Jail** V1 ★★★

___**79. Clink** V0

DYNO ROCK

___**80. Jack Brown** V3

Start on jug by bush; traverse right along seam.

___**81. Mini** V1
Mini-dyno.

___**82. Hot Joint** V2
 Start in crack, look for little Gaston for R; L hits lip.

LEANING ROCK

___**83. Dressed in Black** V2
 Start on big flake; climb out right.

___**84. Leaning Rock** V5★★★
 Same start as #83; L hand rolls up to small crimp; R goes to crimp over lip; climb up face.

BOB

___**85. The Judge** V0

SPEED

___**86. Mercy** V3
 Climbs arête.

CAVE

___**87. The Cave** V5 ★★★
The original start is on the obvious jug. A sit down start has been added. It starts on two underclings down as low as you can get.

THE CRACK

___**88. Harden** V0
Finger crack; short.

EGG

___**89. 99 Years** V0

___**90. Bid** V1
Same start as #89; climb left along crack.

___**91. Heart Broke** V2

___**92. K.G.** V4 ★★
Start on crimps; climb to crack; L hand goes out left to small crimp in lichen; R hits lip.

___**93. 15 Years** V0
Climb dirty crack.

UTE

___**94. Kill Your Enemies** V6 ★★
Starts head height on crimps; big move to lip.

___**95. Grave** V1
Starts on jug above your head.

___**96. Black Rider** V7 ★★
 L Gaston, R Gaston, L goes to undercling out right; pulls lip.

DUFFY ARÊTE

___97. Get-A-Grip V2 ★

Climb arête.

___98. Take Your Money and Run
V2

Small cave to the right.

Note: *There are many more problems above Duffy Arête up in the talus.*

PLATFORM

___99. Lowe V1

___100. Lowe 1 V3 ★★★

Start matching on jug; L to undercling; R to rail finish out left. A to B.

___101. Lowe 2 V3 ★★★

Same start as #100; R to pocket; L to rail. A to C to B.

___102. A. Lowe 3 V4 ★★

Same start as #100. Climbs out right to arête. A to C to D.

___102. B. Lowe 4 V3

Climb up arête; traverse left. E to B.

___102. C. Lowe 5 V1

Climb east arête.

SLAB

___103. Worm V3

Climb west arête.

___104. Don't Want to Grow Up
V7 ★★★

 Starts on west arête; climbs right into #105.

___105. Mule V3 ★★★

Climbs the big features in the middle of the boulder.

___106. Joe Bean V4

Uses arête to right of #103; finish in scoop.

___107. B-Day V3

Climb the groove; funky problem.

Platform Detail

(B) (D) (A) (E) (C) slab

INDEX

INDEX :

OUR ADVERTISERS ROCK

Sharp End Publishing

Authentic Guides From Core Climbers

Book Titles	Retail
Betty and the Silver Spider: Welcome to Gym Climbing	$12.95
Black Canyon Rock Climbs	$28.00
A Bouldering Guide to Utah	$34.95
Castles in the Sand: A Climber's Guide to Sedona and Oak Creek Canyon	$24.95
Classic Boulder Climbs	$9.95
Classic Desert Climbs, 2nd Edition	$14.00
Colorado Bouldering	$28.00
Colorado Bouldering 2	$28.00
Double Down: A Select Guide to Vegas Limestone and Sandstone	$14.00
Enchanted Rock: A Climber's Guide	$16.95
Front Range Topropes	$16.95
A Guide to Rock Climbing in Northern Thailand	$24.95
Indian Creek: A Climbing Guide	$32.95
Jemez Rock	$24.95
The Legendary Wild Iris	$10.00
Life by the Drop: Ice and Mixed Climbs Surrounding CO's San Luis Valley	$14.00
Mountain Biking Colorado's Western Slope	$9.95
Northern Utah Limestone	$16.95
Ogden Area Climbing Guide: From Brigham City to Echo Canyon	$19.95
Oklahoma Select: A Climber's Guide	$16.95
The Park: Climbs of Rocky Mountain National Park	$9.95
Rifle: Climbers' Guide to Rifle Mountain Park	$7.95
The Ripper: Rock, Ice and Bouldering in the Wet Mountains near Pueblo, CO	$14.00
Rock Climbs of Southwest Utah and the Arizona Strip, 2nd Edition	$32.95
The Rock Warrior's Way	$16.95
Sandia Rock	$14.95
Serious Play: An Annotated Guide to Front Range Trad Classics 5.2-5.9	$18.00
Shelf Road Rock: A Complete Climbing Reference	$28.00
South Platte Rock	$12.95
Spearfish Canyon Limestone	$14.95
Sport Climbs of Sinks Canyon	$11.95
Taos Rock: Climbs & Boulders of Northern New Mexico	$19.95
Tuolumne Topropes	$10.95
Winter Trails of the Front Range	$7.95
Yosemite Topropes	$8.95
Zion Rock	$14.00
Annual Women of Climbing Calendar	$15.95

Video Titles

Comfortably Numb (DVD)	$29.95
A Day in the Life: 5 Women Who Climb (DVD)	$24.95
Fitlife Pilates (VHS)	$15.00
Friction Addiction (VHS and DVD)	$30.00
Front Range Freaks (VHS and DVD)	$30.00
Inertia 1 & 2 (DVD)	$24.95
Return2Sender (DVD	$30.00
Scary Faces (VHS)	$30.00

888.594.6398
www.sharpendbooks.com